Karolinum Press

MODERN CZECH CLASSICS

Views from the Inside

Czech Underground Literature and Culture (1948–1989)

Texts by
Ivan M. Jirous,
Paul Wilson, Egon Bondy,
and Jáchym Topol

Edited by
Martin Machovec

KAROLINUM PRESS 2018

KAROLINUM PRESS
Karolinum Press is a publishing department of Charles University
Ovocný trh 560/5, 116 36 Prague 1
Czech Republic
www.karolinum.cz

Texts © 2018 by Egon Bondy (heirs), Ivan M. Jirous (heirs), Jáchym Topol,
Paul Wilson
Translation © 2018 by Ivan Hartel, Tomáš Liška, Gerald Turner, Paul Wilson
Edition and epilogue © 2018 by Martin Machovec

Designed by Zdeněk Ziegler
Set and printed in the Czech Republic by Karolinum Press
Second English edition, first in Karolinum

Cataloging-in-Publication Data is available from the National Library
of the Czech Republic

ISBN 978-80-246-3592-7 (pb)
ISBN 978-80-246-3593-4 (ebk)

CONTENTS

Ivan Martin Jirous
Report on the Third Czech Musical Revival

*In the great cultural revolutions there is only one way for the people –
to free themselves by their own efforts. Nothing must be used that would
do it for them. Believe in people, rely on them and respect their initiative.
Cast away fear! Don't be afraid of commotion. Let people educate
themselves in the great revolutionary movement.*
MAO TSE-TUNG[1]

(I)

At the end of 1974, a day before New Year's Eve, we went by train
to a concert in Líšnice, a small village west of Prague. We got out
at the nearest station and went the remaining few kilometres
on foot, through the dusky, half-frozen muddy fields. There were
about forty-five of us: we knew that another crowd of our friends
were approaching Líšnice from the bus stop on the other side, and
that many more were coming by car. Our mood was one of sheer
joy. There was a tangible hope that we would be celebrating the
end of the year with music: we were going to the first concert of a
group called Umělá Hmota (Artificial Material),[2] and after that the
Plastics and DG 307 were to play. As we walked through the bleak
countryside, many of us experienced an intense feeling, which some
expressed in words. It reminded us of the pilgrimages of the first
Hussites into the mountains. When this was said, we made jokes
along those lines and developed the theme. As soon as we came

1) The epigraph is taken from "Decision of the Central Committee of the Chinese
Communist Party Concerning the Great Proletarian Cultural Revolution", 4, "Let the
Masses Educate Themselves in the Movement." See *Peking Review* 9, no. 33 (1966):
6–11; online at https://www.marxists.org/subject/china/peking-review/1966/PR1966
-33g.htm.
The English translation in the *Peking Review* is a bit different: *"In the Great Proletarian
Cultural Revolution, the only method is for the masses to liberate themselves, and any
method of doing things in their stead must not be used. Trust the masses, rely on them
and respect their initiative. Cast out fear. Don't be afraid of disturbances. Chairman Mao
has often told us that revolution cannot be so very refined, so gentle, so temperate, kind,
courteous, restrained and magnanimous. Let the masses educate themselves in this great
revolutionary movement and learn to distinguish between right and wrong and between
correct and incorrect ways of doing things."*
2) Sometimes translated as Artificial Matter or Synthetic Material.

to Líšnice, we said, the lords – today the establishment – would be waiting to drive us away.

And that was what happened. In spite of the fact that the concert was sponsored by a group of local firemen (with whom the musicians often play football), in spite of the fact that local council had approved the event, we were told to disperse at once, or else force would be used. We dispersed, because today people who want to listen to the music they like (just like the people in the days of Hus who went to the hills to listen to words they wanted to hear) have no other recourse for the time being but to retreat from violence. As we were leaving the hall in the Líšnice restaurant, there was a party of hunters in the next room with a brass band that produced as many decibels as a rock group, and there they were celebrating the New Year under a decorated evergreen, that loving symbol of Christmas. One member of this group was the man who forbade others to enjoy themselves in the way they wanted. Arrogantly, he refused to speak to any of us and called the police. He was vice-chairman of the local council.

In the past, they would have called him a servant of the Anti-Christ; today, he is a representative of the establishment. He doesn't deserve the attention he is getting here. He is just one of the many nameless bureaucrats who, since the beginning of the seventies, have frustrated, banned or broken up many such musical gatherings. He is symptomatic of a time that turns its hatred and suspicion against people who desire nothing more than to create the type of art and environment that they must create, who stubbornly refuse to let their art be used in any other way than to speak to those who, with the artists, wish to live in truth.

(II)

I am not as interested in describing what these people do – for the music must be heard to be appreciated – as I am in explaining how and why they do it. I have called it the third Czech musical revival, a period that began in early 1970s, most probably about 1973.

It is not important when the first Czech musical revival took place (if there ever was one): our term comes from a statement once made by Karel Voják, a friend of the Primitives Group. He referred to the late sixties as the "second musical revival", a time when there was an unexpected boom in rock music (or Big Beat, as they called it then) – mainly in Prague, but elsewhere in Bohemia as well.

In Prague alone, there were several hundred rock groups. Few of them achieved public recognition, let alone fame. But that's not the point. The most important thing was their sheer numbers. For the first time, people who would normally have no access to art – because of their social origins, their ignorance of what education is, or their unwillingness to continue in school, given the difficulty of getting a real education in the present school system – now had this opportunity. And regardless of quality, the profusion of these groups made natural selection possible. Bands formed, played, disbanded and regrouped into new ones. How else can people with similar opinions and natures get to know about each other except when they can display what they know in a relatively public forum?

I consider one of the greatest crimes of the present establishment to be the information blockade surrounding young people at that most important age – from 16 to 19 years of age – when their minds are taking definitive shape. I get furious when I hear people saying that anyone who really wants to achieve something can do it, regardless of the obstacles. Where are these young people and how can one find what they are looking for when they are being surrounded by an impenetrable wall of silence and misinformation? Josef Janíček, now the bandmaster of The Plastic People, played with group called The Swimmers for three years before joining The Primitives Group at the age of 19. Milan Hlavsa first performed with The Undertakers and two other short-lived bands that he had established, The New Electric Potatoes and Hlavsa's Fiery Factory, before forming The Plastic People of the Universe in September 1968 at the age of 19. How can the people in Czechoslovakia today form bands with a decent chance for survival when there is no spontaneous musical milieu in which they can meet, compare notes, play together, or follow their own path while being guided by their own freely felt musical sense and, above all, by a feeling of kinship? But whatever the case, those times are gone forever. The main purpose of this brief excursion into the history of Czech rock music is to make a comparison with the present state of things, which I will deal with shortly. I have deliberately not mentioned the names of any once-famous Czech rock bands; my point was rather to draw attention to the vast range of the music existing at that time. There was however one band in Prague that cannot be overlooked: The Primitives Group.

(III)

When the mode of the music changes
When the mode of the music changes
The walls of the city shake.
THE FUGS[3]

Now that some years have gone by, we can say without exaggeration that the appearance of The Primitives Group in Prague marked the arrival of a new phenomenon – underground music – even though it was emotionally and instinctively, rather than consciously understood. This is another reason why I have not mentioned other bands from the "golden" era of Czech rock: lamentably, they blew their opportunities and responsibilities. It was amazing to see how younger musicians far outdid their colleagues in older, degenerated forms of music, in terms of commercializing and marketing their music. How their sole aim became a career in small musical clubs and theatres and how they made great efforts to conventionalize their performances so that they could not be attacked by the weak-minded critics who judged rock music by dead standards that no longer applied to anything, not even to those fields of art from which they had originally been borrowed.

In this commercial sea of mental poverty into which one officially accepted band after another submerged itself, the Primitives Group could not be overlooked. It was a rough-hewn group, miles away from the artificial smoothness of other bands, and in fact was probably unconsciously trying for precisely this effect. It did not have its own repertoire but proved its sensitivity by playing music by Jimi Hendrix, Eric Burdon, The Grateful Dead, The Pretty Things, The

---

3) The song is from the Fugs album *It Crawled into my Hand, Honest* (1968).

Doors, The Mothers of Invention, and The Fugs. In the late sixties, the performance of English and American rock by Czech groups was absolutely essential in the local scene. At that time the market was far less flooded with foreign records than it is today. Back then, when The Primitives Group first played Zappa, he was familiar only to a handful of people.

But that alone would not have been enough to make The Primitives Group the legitimate fathers of the underground as a movement that has created, outside of a corrupt society, its own independent world with a different charge of inner energy, different aesthetic and, as a result, a different ethic. What made them unique was their emphasis on one stream of contemporary music which was at that time called *psychedelic sound*. In this respect The Primitives Group were quite original and creative, if only because at the time they knew little more about it than what the expression "psychedelic sound" meant; nevertheless, they captured its proper spirit. Through their music they tried to create in their listeners a particular mental state which, temporarily at least, liberated them and exposed the primary foundation of their being. They used other means besides music to achieve this – approaches borrowed from art and, above all, from happenings – in concerts like FISH FEAST (celebrating water), BIRD FEAST (air) and others using fire. In brief, as soon as the official critics of pop music began to pay attention to this *enfant terrible* of Czech rock, the group voluntarily disbanded. This did not mean the end of psychedelic music in Prague, however. When The Primitives Group split up in April 1969, The Plastic People of the Universe had already been playing together for five months.

(IV)
The world is beautiful
But plastic people don't see it.
Flowers are beautiful
But plastic people don't see it.
The sunset is beautiful
But plastic people don't see it.
There is only one thing for their eyes
Only one thing is beautiful to them:
Plastic People in the Underground.
THE UNIVERSE SYMPHONY

The Plastic People of the Universe took up the banner of the underground consciously but, just as The Primitives Group created their own version of psychedelic music out of lack of knowledge and information, the Plastics understood the term "underground" purely in terms of feeling, an essentially literal interpretation of the word. One important factor for the development of rock music in Prague was the fact that the founder of The Plastic People, Milan Hlavsa, was an excellent composer. Original music was combined with original texts which, in the first place (let's call it the mythological phase of the Plastics) reflected a kind of cosmology of the underground. In this period, the underground was understood in mythological terms of the world as an alternative mentality different from the mentality of people living in the establishment. The lyrics of Michal Jernek and Věra Jirousová, full of echoes from the Cabbala of Cornelius Agrippa of Nettesheim (whose symbols were used by The Primitives Group in their celebrations of the elements), often presented attitudes of people of the underground that fully justified the addition "of the Universe" in the group's name. In a song characteristic of that period, *The Sun*, the Plastics sang: "All the stupid brains are out in the sun; our powerful nation lives in a velvet underground". In the composition *The Universe Symphony*, they celebrated the individual planets of the solar system; the section devoted to Earth was called *Plastic People Underground*. In *The Song of Two Unearthly Worlds*, about the mythic Fafejta Bird, there are references not only to Celtic mythology and the Agrippan Cabbala, but also to the world of rock music (John Lennon and Yoko Ono) which, again, was presented through mythological interpretation. Even when the Plastics turned to the real world, as it might seem in the song *Fireball* – which celebrates one of their favourite figures in Czech history, Prokop Diviš, the eccentric inventor of the lighting rod – the facts of the story were so radically altered (Diviš is sitting in a cabin inside the Canadian woods with his friends, one of which is Roy Estrada, a former bass guitarist of The Mothers of Invention) that it was clear they were once again interpreting reality using mythical terms.

The Plastic People consciously continued a tradition established by The Primitives Group through their use of visual techniques to strengthen the impact of their music. Costumed attendants guarded fires burning on stage, the members of the band played with painted faces, and, in the composition of *Fireball*, there was a fire-eater performance. At the premiere of *The Universe Symphony* in the artists' club in Mánes in Prague, the Plastics killed a live chicken as a sacrifice to the god Mars. During the same evening (this was shortly after man had first landed on the Moon), they burned the model flying saucer that had always been an essential part of their stage decoration.

Along with their own work, the Plastic People continued the tradition of "enlightenment" established by The Primitives Group: they were the first group to present to Czech audience live performances of work by Warhol's group The Velvet Underground and the vast majority of songs by Ed Sanders and Tuli Kupferberg of The Fugs from New York. Of course, they also performed new works by Zappa.

That was roughly the situation at the time when the tag "of the Universe" was fully justified. The Plastics still bear their full name today, out of a fidelity to their original title. Nonetheless, things that have happened since then firmly anchored them to earth. The mythological underground has become a genuine sociological and cultural underground, in the sense proclaimed in the early sixties by Ed Sanders, Allen Ginsberg, Jeff Nuttall, Timothy Leary, and many other pioneers of this movement. I would even go so far as to say that, in relation to our establishment, it has become an underground in the true sense of the word.

(V)

Again, the devil took him to a very high mountain and showed him
all the kingdoms of the world and the glory of them; and he said to him,
"All these I will give you, if you will fall down and worship me."
THE GOSPEL ACCORDING TO ST. MATTHEW, 4, 8-9

At the beginning of the 1970s, the establishment took drastic steps which, practically speaking, destroyed rock music as a movement. Groups were forbidden to have repertoires sung in English, bands with English names were forced to change them, and many top rock musicians deplorably became back-up musicians for the stars of commercial pop music. The Plastic People of the Universe decided to reject all the changes enforced on them by an alien will that did not flow naturally from the character and inner needs of the musicians. They kept their name, their repertoire and their appearance intact. The group lost its professional status; weaker individuals left and the core of the new Plastic People – around Hlavsa and Janíček – started off practically empty-handed with no equipment, only a few instruments and apparently nothing to fall back on but the absolutely clear concept that it is the musician's responsibility to play the kind of music that his conscience tells him to play and that gives him pleasure, for this is the only way that he can share his creative joy with his audience.

After a period of public inactivity during which the newly formed Plastic People were consolidated and joined by the excellent violinist Jiří Kabeš (Paul Wilson sang with them for some time), they began to perform at occasional dances. When playing in Ledeč nad Sázavou in the winter of 1971, it was already clear to people that it was an important rock group that proved one could survive without making compromises. Dozens of people came to Ledeč from Prague, Karlsbad and other cities. The mood that was later described as "going into the mountains" (as I mentioned in the introduction) began to take shape. When Milan Hlavsa saw all the people in Ledeč who hitch-hiked or travelled long distances by car, train or bus to hear the Plastic People performing, he made a memorable statement: "We couldn't just shit on these people, even if we wanted to. What kind of entertainment would they have left if we had done so?"

The Plastic People found themselves in the exceptional position of being the only underground rock group in Bohemia. Their whole existence showed that "underground" was not just an attractive label indicating a certain musical tendency, but that it presented, above all, an attitude towards life.

I have always felt angry towards other relatively decent rock groups who in the early 1970s were trying to make an official name for themselves and surrendered to the demands of the establishment in exchange for the right to play publicly music, **some kind of music**, thus making it impossible for themselves to be truly creative.

Why did these musicians do it? I think it was because they lacked, and they are still lacking, the awareness of what art is, what function it has in the world, and what responsibilities those who were awarded the gift of creativity should have. Anyone who is not absolutely clear about that in his own mind can easily fall off track. The Plastic People maintained their integrity not because they were good musicians – in other rock groups of the time, there were better musicians – yet during the most difficult period, when they were lacking equipment, had nothing to fall back on and no public prospects, one thing was clear to them: **It is better not to play at all than to play music that does not flow from one's own convictions. It is better not to play at all than to play what the establishment demands**. And even this statement appears too mild. It is not better; it is absolutely essential. This stand must be taken right at the beginning. For as soon as the first compromise is made, whether it is accompanied by hypocritical excuses or it springs from an honest belief that it doesn't really matter, everything is lost.

As soon as the devil (who today speaks through the mouth of the establishment) lays down the first condition: cut your hair, just a little, and you'll be able to play – you must say no. As soon as the devil (who today speaks through the mouth of the establishment) says – change your name and you'll be able to continue playing what you've been playing – you must say no, we will not play at all.

At the same time it is not even a real issue, for the establishment has no power to prevent from playing those who reject all the advantages that follow from being professional musicians. The establishment can only put pressure on those who want to be better off than the rest. For those who want to live a better life – not in the sense of financial security, but in terms directed towards the following of the truth – the long arm of the establishment is too short. Only those artists who understand that they were awarded with the gift of art with the help of which they may speak to those close to them and will not use it to become better off than the rest deserve to be called artists. "The great artist of tomorrow will go underground", wrote Marcel Duchamp at the end of his life.[4] He didn't use the word "underground" to indicate some new trend. He meant the underground as a new mental attitude of an honest artist who reacts against the dehumanization and prostitution of values in the consumer society.

(VI)

The claim that the Plastic People became the only genuinely underground rock group in Czechoslovakia does not indicate that they were the only underground music group to exist. A band called Aktual performed alongside the Plastic People for a short time. Although it could be loosely defined as a rock band, its leader and composer, Milan Knížák, employed techniques of aleatoric music and serial composition (and while doing so he declared his affinity with the new music represented above all by John Cage). Knížák, who was primarily involved with happenings, environments and

---

4) See Paul Bennett, "Marcel Duchamp, un art de vivre", from LE DEVOIR.com (<http://www.ledevoir.com/2007/07/14/150252.html>): "Duchamp fustigera jusqu'à la fin de sa vie l'ego des artistes et la compétition dans le domaine de l'art. Pour lui, l'artiste véritable ne peut que se réfugier dans la clandestinité, aller sous terre pour échapper à la frénésie de l'art commercialisé. Il fut un des premiers, sinon le premier, à utiliser le terme d'»underground«: »The great artist of tomorrow will go underground«, déclara-t-ill à la occasion d'un colloque organisé en 1961 par le Musée de Philadelphie, qui avait hérité de la collection la plus complète de ses oeuvres /.../."
See also Jean Neyens 1965 interview with Duchamp: (<http://toutfait.com/duchamp.jsp?postid=1440&keyword=>): "Une table ronde qu'on avait faite à Philadelphie, on m'avait demandé »Ou allons-nous?« Moi j'ai simplement dit: »Le grand bonhomme de demain se cachera. Ira sous terre.« En anglais c'est mieux qu'en français – »Will go underground«. Il faudra qu'il meure avant d'être connu. Moi, c'est mon avis, s'il y a un bonhomme important d'ici un siècle ou deux – eh bien! Il se sera caché toute sa vie pour échapper à l'emprise du marché... complètement mercantile, si j'ose dire." (Duchamp refers here to the year 1961.)

events was somewhat ahead of his time when establishing this band. Unlike the Plastic People, he did not have a wide public ready to accept his music. (In this respect, the slow process of educating an audience to accept new musical forms – which had been going on since the era of the Primitives Group – proved its legacy). It resulted in a strange paradox: in October 1971, when Aktual and the Plastic People performed together in Suchá, a few hundred young people listened to the Plastics with enthusiasm (at that time their repertoire consisted almost entirely of songs of the Velvet Underground, along with several of their own compositions), but Aktual flopped. The only ones who liked Knížák's music were the Plastic People themselves and their immediate circle.

They were delighted by the energy, liveliness and variety of Aktual's performance in which the members of the band used empty tar-barrels, motorcycle, electric drills, axes, chopping blocks, rice, etc. What impressed them the most, however, were Knížák's lyrics[5] in Czech which communicated provocative ideas directly to an audience which had so far been used to hearing songs in English (the lingua franca of rock). It is true, of course, that from the very beginning the Plastic People had some Czech songs in their repertoire but they were all performed as recitatives that had a tendency to intensify the bizarre and manneristic side of the Plastics' performances, rather than addressing people directly. Knížák, on the other hand, was firmly convinced – at a time when the notion was still far from popular – that contemporary music ought to speak to people in the language they understand.

Precisely because I value very highly Knížák's influence on the evolution of Plastic People – it was not a direct influence, but rather an impulse that came from the revealing comparison Aktual offered – I must mention an inherent weakness that we observed in Knížák's group and which later clearly led to its collapse. It has to do with the contradictions in Knížák's personality. Though he has always proclaimed that art should be almost an anonymous activity (in his case he and his collaborators were concealed behind the

---

5) Some of Milan Knížák's lyrics written for the band Aktual, both in Czech original and in English translation, were published in a booklet added to the CD *Aktual: děti bolševizmu / Kids of Bolshevism*, Guerrilla Records, 2005).

collective name Aktual), in reality he has remained individualistic, a leader, an almost hypnotizing personality towering far above those around him. Except for the drummer and flutist of the group, Jan Maria Mach, Knížák used other members of the group as musical instruments on which he himself played through the power of his mind and will. The result was undoubtedly impressive, and the method certainly worked as far as the concrete, musical results are concerned, but it is not sufficient enough in situations where the interests of survival demand a group of equally important individuals, whose mutual interaction produces unified work. This, in fact, is what Knížák himself proclaims. But once again I must point out the paradoxical relationship between the Plastic People and Aktual: it seems incontestable that Aktual indirectly influenced the development of the Plastic People, but, to close the circle, I think the wide community that today exists around the Plastic People of the Universe has in fact created what Aktual dealt with only in symbolic terms. (See their song *There'll be a town of the Aktuals*.)

(VII)

From a certain point on, there is no longer any going back.
And that point must be reached.[6]
FRANZ KAFKA

Even by the time the Plastic People had become an underground band in the social and cultural sense, something of a lyrical note survived in their repertoire. They set to music poems by William Blake, a text from the *Faerie Queene* by Edmund Spenser (the same text that Henry Purcell set to music centuries before) and poems by Jiří Kolář from his romantic, post-war period. This was not without importance, either for the band or for its audiences. It drew people's attention to the fact that contemporary rock music was not something that fell out of a clear blue sky, something completely cut off from

6) Jirous quotes from Franz Kafka, *Aforismy*, translated from German to Czech by Rio Preisner (Prague: Československý spisovatel, 1968, p. 7).
American poet and translator Geoffrey Brock renders the line as, "Beyond a certain point there's no return. That is the point that must be reached," in his translation of Roberto Calasso's *K.* (New York: Knopf, 2005).

the cultural heritage of Western Civilization of which we are a part. But the core of their repertoire, with the exception of Kolář's poems, was still sung in English and the band – particularly its *spiritus agens* Milan Hlavsa – began to feel more and more that this was a handicap.

The final impulse that the Plastic People needed to become troubadours was an encounter with the work of the poet Egon Bondy, and from then on, with some exceptions, they have exclusively set his poems to music. Bondy is a poet who deals with the most basic and profound aspects of man, from his dimensions as a social creature to his imperfect and very vulnerable private biological being. In his poetry he has instinctively fulfilled one point of the programme set forth by representatives of the underground in 1964: "To uproot absolutely, and once for all, the Pauline lie which silently assumes, in Christian convention, that people do not shit, do not piss, and do not screw".[7] There is hardly a single taboo that is not overturned in Bondy's poetry; but this is never done as an end in itself or as a deliberate provocation: it is merely a simple expression of the truth of life and the position of man in the world. By setting to music the work of a poet who was not allowed by the establishment to publish even a single poem, the Plastic People were clearly demonstrating that they were not interested in gaining a place in the official cultural structure but far more in creating and acting as a medium for what they themselves consider culture.

By this time the core of the group was strong enough to be characterized in definite terms. The members complemented each other in an extraordinary way: the restless spirit of Milan Hlavsa with his irrepressible tendency to push forward the development of his music; Josef Janíček, a many-sided musician with a remarkable inner discipline who forms a kind of stable antipole to Hlavsa's mercurial nature; Jiří Kabeš who played in a rock'n'roll band at the very beginning of Czech rock music in the early 1960s and then, after several years of inactivity, joined the Plastics at their invitation – the harsh sound of his viola adds a rather otherworldly feeling to Hlavsa's compositions; and finally, the saxophonist Vratislav Brabenec with his spontaneity and, above all, humour which adds so much to the musical setting of Bondy's poetry.

---

7) See Jeff Nuttall, *Bomb Culture* (New York: Delacorte Press, 1968, p. 264).

Even at the point when the Plastic People were singing lyrics that spoke directly to the audiences, they did not ignore the theatrical aspects of their performances, which often, in part at least, became musical happenings. At the end of their concert in Klukovice in June 1973, they played a number called *How It Will Be After Death*[8] (after a short story of the same name by the Czech philosopher Ladislav Klíma) – an aleatoric-electronic composition using that strange instrument the theremin. A huge banner hiding the musicians was stretched across the stage with the words *And Wandered I Round Fields Five* (the key quotation from Klíma's story) on it. The poet Pavel Zajíček, who stood on a table leering at the audience over the banner with a light bulb in front of his mouth, finished the song by leaping headlong through the banner into the audience on the floor in front of the podium.

The most effective piece of scenic business was at a concert of the Plastic People in Veleň near Prague in December 1973. In complete contrast to the usual atmosphere of rock music events, the whole thing was done in the style of country brass band dances. An environment was created on the stage with an enormous tangle of hornbeam branches. The musicians sat on tree-stumps quietly eating their lunch, drinking beer and talking among themselves as though the audience didn't exist. Pavel Zajíček stood on one side of the stage wearing a silver asbestos heat suit[9] and shouting a dream he had the night before into the microphone: "The first of December! Plastic People of the Universe concertino! December 26, everybody into the mountains with a bag of beans! Anti! Stick your head out of the pillow – throw off your burden at last – get rid of the terrible ruler – cast off those kilos of paranoia – go – drink – barf – live – drink – dink! I run against the screen with a handful of shit; I plaster the shit right into it". Then he began shouting "Anti Anti!", repeating it over and over again in slow, rhythmic and monotonous tones, broken occasionally by shouts of "DG 307 greets Praguers!

---

8) Translated by Marek Tomin as *Afterlife* in the book *The Plastic People of the Universe* (Prague: Globus Music-Maťa, 1999).
9) The heat suit was actually used by a Czech mountaineering expedition exploring the volcanoes of Ecuador [author's note].

Aunty Hendrix, the common wayfarer from Ostroh – Seeberg!"[10] The obvious contradictions between his schizoid performance and what was occurring on the stage behind him where the musicians, ignoring him completely, ate their lunch and then gradually began to sing the song *Do lesíčka na čekanou* out of tune, the way the song can be heard in pubs just before closing time, is analogous to the way the Plastic People put their lyrics to music. They reserve the sweetest melodies for lyrics like "Yesterday, on Sunday, I had an awfully itchy arse".[11] The provocative tension created by the contrast between the crudeness of the lyrics and the beauty of the music is one of the most powerful aspects of psychedelic music. When the Plastics at last began to play, the puzzled audience did not hear the rock music it had been prepared to hear, but a series of electronic compositions that were almost like happenings (for example, *Kohoutek's Comet*, in which Ivo Pospíšil of DG 307 walked up and down the stage in a star-studded gown carrying a toy comet on a stick, while Hlavsa crowed like a rooster [*Kohoutek* means little rooster in Czech]). After several songs of a more traditional nature, the set was concluded with the theme-song *Do lesíčka...*, in which the basic brass-band melody was taken up by the viola interrupted by the other instruments in the counter-rhythms of traditional rock music.

In spite of the aspects of electronic music that the Plastic People absorbed both from sensitive listening to contemporary rock (Zappa and Captain Beefheart) and from what they learned from Edgar Varèse, in spite of some aleatonic approaches, and in spite of the hints of jazz that Brabenec brought into the group, the essence of the Plastic People's music remains a lively and emphatic rock rhythm which has become cultivated today, being sometimes almost manneristic but never academic. However, the fundamental characteristic of their music is their use of the human voice as an instrument with which to address people. It is probably no accident that in most of the more interesting Czech and Slovak rock groups,

10) At this time, Zajíček and Hendrix and others were living together in an old castle called Seeberg in Western Bohemia, where they were trying to form a commune [author's note].
11) Translated as *Yesterday On Sunday* by Marek Tomin (see *The P. P. o. U.*, 1999, p. 62): "Yesterday on Sunday / my bum was really itchy / The reason was the way / I'd stuffed myself all day".

instrumental compositions predominate. The voice articulating something is dangerous and bands that do not want to sing degenerated lyrical nonsense or do not have the courage (or have never had the idea) to sing lyrics that genuinely communicate something to people, solve the problem by leaving the voice out altogether.

Precisely by emphasizing the voice and its message The Plastic People of the Universe – in spite of the richness and complexity of their music – are far closer to bands like the Fugs or David Peel's Lower East Side than to, for example, Zappa's Mothers of Invention in their instrumental period.

(VIII)

I think that 1973 marked the beginning of the third revival of Czech music. Why? First of all, two new bands were formed at that time – the Midsummer Night's Dream Band and DG 307. At the same time, communal events began to take place in which bands with differing musical orientations participated; the intolerance that existed between rock music and other musical forms disappeared and people began to pay more attention to the things that bound them together in opposition to the cultural policies of the establishment than to differences in taste and aversions to various types of artistic expression.

In the spring of 1973, a member of the Crusaders' School[12] from one of the western countries was on a visit to Prague; for the last few years he had been coming to Prague almost every year and this time he spoke of his surprise at how serious we had all become. He knew us as a reckless, spontaneous lot and, all of a sudden, he found small groups of people who had somehow – at least this was

---

12) The Crusaders' School of Pure Humour Without Jokes: *Křižovnická škola čistého humoru bez vtipu*, a loose group of artists of the 60s and early 70s, of which I. M. Jirous was a member, was named after the Prague pub "U křižovníků", their meeting-place. See the Czech catalogue *K. Š. Křižovnická škola čistého humoru bez vtipu* (Hradec Králové-Prague: Galerie moderního umění, 1991). The mentioned "member [...] from one of the western countries" was, according to Paul Wilson, the Canadian actor and a playwright, Ted Johns. See also the Czech catalogue *Křižovnická škola čistého humoru bez vtipu* (Roudnice nad Labem: Galerie moderního umění v Roudnici, 2015, ed. Duňa Slavíková).

how he put it – become more intellectual. We needed this view from the outside to become aware of how weary we had all grown since 1969. It was a time when we all began to realize that the situation we were living in was not temporary, that it would last for a long time, probably forever. It was definitely a rather dead period as far as our collective activities were concerned; a time of muteness and hangover as far as the official cultural situation was concerned, at least compared to how it seemed at the beginning of the 1970s. I have a feeling that 1973 was a decisive year in overcoming that crisis. People had to stop relying on the fact that something would once again enable musicians to play, poets to publish and artists to exhibit. Relying on miracles cripples creative energy and, above all, weakens collective activity: one is dominated by the feeling that nothing which seems impossible is worth doing. But the conscious realization or the subconscious sense that something is here for good is necessarily liberating. If the world is never going to be any different than it is now, there is no need to waste your time waiting for salvation. We must learn to live in the existing world in a way that is both joyful and dignified.

(IX)

The Midsummer Night's Dream Band started as the band of the Crusaders' School of Pure Humour Without Jokes; it was formed by three artists – Karel Nepraš, Míla Hájek and Milan Čech, chemical engineer Petr Lampl, and the multi-faceted musician Vráťa Brabenec who also played with the Plastic People. Nepraš's presence in the band is no accident and to a certain extent determined the continuity and direction that the band took; for just as Nepraš's activity in the Crusaders' School is an extension of what he did in the neo-Dadaist group called the Šmidras in the early 1960s, so the Midsummer Night's Dream band occupies a similar position as the Šmidra brass band did in the Prague cultural world. Its members were all avant-garde painters and sculptors at that time. It is significant that while Nepraš's former friends from the Šmidras now hold "Millionaire Parties" attended by people like Helena Vondráčková and other representatives of official pop music, Nepraš is one of the founding members of the group in which the true spirit of the Šmidras still lives on. Let us leave aside speculation about how these snobs who are being addressed by other Šmidras today value their activity. What is more interesting for us is how the Midsummer Night's Dream Band is received by people who until recently rejected any music except rock. At *Soukup's Marriage*, a riverboat outing arranged by the Plastic People and their friends in June 1973, the Midsummer Night's Dream Band was received with spontaneous enthusiasm.

This band fulfils one of the basic needs of any freethinking person – the need for humour. With a perfect sense of mimicry and in utter seriousness modified only by deliberate faults in the music – they perform famous works of classical music (Mozart's *Eine Kleine Nachtmusik*) and notorious pop hits like the themes from Dr. Zhivago and the music of Johann Strauss, in a highly personal way, often integrating both genres in a single performance. The young audience has accepted the Midsummer Night's Dream Band as one of its favourite bands because it was sensitively attuned to the authenticity of this grotesque musical phenomenon that could never be appreciated by any contemporary musical critic.

Among the most famous events undertaken by the Midsummer Night's Dream were two happenings arranged by Olaf Hanel. On the second day of spring 1973, they went to Blaník where, on the natural podium that formed the top of the legendary hill, the band played for the Blaník knights [according to the legend, the knights of Blaník are sleeping inside the hill, waiting to be woken up when the nation is in mortal danger]. A year later, when the Year of Czech Music was being celebrated all over the world, the Midsummer Night's Dream Band and their friends drove in a rented bus to the Vltava river springs and back and on the way they played themes from Smetana's symphonic poem *Vltava* in appropriate locations.

The Midsummer Night's Dream Band has undoubtedly its place in the broad spectrum of neo-Dadaist phenomenon, a common feature in the art of the past thirty years. Nonetheless, at this moment an obvious shift in meaning has taken place when compared with the times when such things were aimed at a narrow intellectual elite. This apparently exclusive or semi-private affair is not directed at individuals but at a wide forum of people who feel that a sense of spiritual kinship is not communicated so much through a particular musical style or trend, as it is through the attitudes of the people who create music towards the establishment and, through the sincerity of their relationships, to each other.

In spite of the delight that the Midsummer Night's Dream Band provides to those who can hear it and see it, we must be aware of its place in today's musical context and of its limitations. It is not a band that could transform people's consciousness or have any fundamental impact on their thinking. It is essentially something very private. This is not a criticism of the band members. As we have seen, the centre of gravity of their work is somewhere else. After all, Karel Nepraš is primarily a sculptor and cartoonist and in these activities, his humour – which manifests itself in its more human form in the band – becomes exceedingly important as it draws our attention to the deformation and hidden terror in human relationships. The Midsummer Night's Dream Band gives its listeners a joyous space in which a game that is unrestrained and uncommitted can be played. How rare and necessary this is in the rigid world in which we must live! However, for music that addresses us with more power and fury, we must turn elsewhere: to DG 307.

(X)

DG 307 was formed sometime in mid-1973 as the offspring of the spiritual symbiosis of two friends, Milan Hlavsa and Pavel Zajíček. It was not born out of any intellectual aim but rather from a boundless spontaneity. Hlavsa's musical schizophrenia is remarkable. The music that he composed for Zajíček's lyrics is entirely different from the music of the Plastic People. He seems to be almost bound by his own musical development (which today has reached almost manneristic dimensions without, however, losing its original power and vitality). If today the Plastic People are treading dangerously close to serious music, DG 307 is more youthful, far more liberated from the conventions of rock or any other type of music. This is further emphasized by the untraditional instruments they use (they play on iron bars, vacuum cleaner tubes, typewriters, etc). A great deal of space is left for accident – and this aspect is reinforced by the large turnover of musicians who complement the two principal members. When working with text, Hlavsa moves between clarity and an attempt to communicate the words clearly (as in *Purification*) to a style that disintegrates the text into syllables which are used as sound so that it becomes impossible to understand it without being familiar with the written text beforehand (as in the *The Drowned Man*).

Likewise, Zajíček's lyrics oscillate between black humour, offering qualified insights into the life of a social outsider and alcoholic,[13] and precise descriptions of the position of people living underground in a consumer society, in which they officially play the role of more or less harmless madmen and fools, but in reality they function as its bad conscience. Recently, much of the humour has disappeared from DG 307. In the group's short lifetime, Zajíček seems to have aged more than it is biologically possible. He has become a chiliastic preacher challenging us in a language that, in spite of his slang, neologisms and Zajíček's own effort to speak naturally, shows the influence of his reading of the New Testament. He speaks to all of us who are determined to live and create in the underground so as not to lose our courage and humanity.

The name DG 307 is a diagnostic code number chosen by the group under the false impression that it meant schizophrenia. In fact, it stands for a "temporary situational disturbances", a diagnosis that is far more accurate as the expression of the position of the band and its circle in the world. The complete diagnosis goes as follows:

"This designation includes all temporary situational disturbances among individuals with no determinable history of mental illness such as the following:
- extreme reaction to stress (panic)
- battle fatigue
- disturbances in the adaptive capacity during adolescence and during old age
- impulsive behaviour
- psychopathic reactions from normal personalities under heavy stress."

DG is the desperate cry of normal people who are incapable of adjusting to the world presented to them by contemporary consumer

---

13) An example of such lyrics is given here in the Czech original: "Když tě čapne / ranní svěrák / myslíš že / vysvobodil by tě / smrťák / kterej tě sekne / do tejla / todle známe dobře / voba dva / Já i Mejla / Já i Pavel".

society. Their compositions might be compared to the early work of the Fugs; but beneath the wild exterior, there lies a deeper gravity that we inherited from the traditions of Central European culture. If DG 307 cries, "We are the symbol of degeneration", it is not merely black humour, it is, as well, testimony of the self-awareness of a generation to which this music belongs. Undoubtedly it is decadent music, in the best sense of the word. But what other kind of progressive music – if we consider true progressiveness to be an adequate response to the world as it presents itself to us – can possibly arise in the environment which we are given to live in?

In contrast to the Plastic People who created and still create a concrete space in which people of good will can encounter one another (even the existence of DG 307 itself is a product of this), the aleatoric nature of DG 307 may also contain the possibility of the absence of such encounters. But even if DG 307 decided to stop playing – for a shorter period or forever – they have already written an unforgettable chapter in the history of the Prague underground movement and Prague rock bands. Even if it was only a shout, we will be hearing its echo for a long time to come.

(XI)
Someday everyone will make art.[14]
COMTE DE LAUTRÉAMONT

When I heard Lautréamont's famous statement for the first time years ago, I could hardly agree with it. This was probably caused by my unconscious feeling of elitism, which is a common disease of intellectuals, and by the source of distrust in the notion that every person has the potential to express himself through an unrepeatable, individual creative act. Today the meaning of the statement has become clear to me: the indispensable condition for liberating the hidden creative potential in any individual is an area of freedom in which he or she lives without any restrictions or prohibitions. If this is not, in general, the case of the contemporary musical scene in

14) See Comte de Lautréamont, *Poésies* II; "La poésie doit être faite par tous, non par un."

Prague, one of the characteristic features of the community around the Plastic People and DG 307 is the openness and lack of suspicion with which it accepts things that would have been almost certainly condemned by those who put technical skill above authenticity and honesty of expression – by technical skill they mean the ability of the artist to tailor his forms of expression to what is already approved or accepted as art.

I refer to the group called Umělá Hmota (Artificial Material). Like the Plastic People, its music is neither polished nor integrated, nor does it express such an aggressive challenge as the music of DG 307. The best way to describe it might be to refer to it as the folklore of the underground; and this only goes to prove the fact that genuine folk art always arises in an environment where there is a sufficiently stimulating creative atmosphere formed by the presence of so-called higher art forms. It is not so important that this new group has many glaring faults, which were unintentionally described with innocent sophistication by the leader of the group as following: "Tuning up is a luxury of bourgeois music." Importantly, it did not appear on the scene as a cold corpse, which often happens to many official rock groups, but as a warm body full of life and expression and, above all, as a body with a voice which has something to say to anyone who listens closely.

Although one could find some shortcomings in the music of Umělá Hmota, if one is willing to take the effort, the group's lyrics are remarkable. They are perfect illustrations of what Jiří Kolář once called urban folklore, especially in the song about the artificial woman *Barbara* or the piece called *The Most Beautiful Girl in the Underground* in which everyday life in Prague is seen through attentive eyes. All members of the group were born in Prague into simple working-class families and did not complete even the basic level of education. Nonetheless, songs like *The End of the World* or *Uncertainties*, in which there are clear echoes of Czech baroque folk literature, which the author of the lyrics has most likely never heard of, take us elsewhere – into the chiliastic atmosphere of Prague underground music.

There are more than just bands in the underground musical scene. At *Hanibal's Wedding* – the first Musical Festival of the Second Culture in September 1974 – two singers appeared, Charlie Soukup and Svatopluk Karásek.

Soukup sings about food, television, football, radio; there is not one sacred issue connected to consumer society that he leaves in peace. But his songs are not like usual songs. Soukup's attitude is not one of protest, but rather of irony. He is not a loudmouth critic, but a subtle commentator on the thick-headedness of all those who have chosen the self-indulgence of the herd over the possibility of being free and diverse people – and thus, above all – of being human.

There are those who describe the audiences at The Plastic People concerts as riff-raff and scum (such as the district judge in České Budějovice), and even those who claim they are not even human beings (as some police officers said after a concert in the workers' club of a large factory in Prague).[15] These people might well be surprised to see the attention and enthusiasm with which this audience receives the songs of Sváťa Karásek which are all, with one exception, religious. Karásek usually begins with the first verse and the melody of spirituals sung in English. It is followed by Czech lyrics which develop from sound associations of the original English words (e.g. "Angel roll that stone away" – "Já jsem ňákej stounavej"). The texts are most effective, however, where the meaning of the original English text and the new Czech version support each other both semantically and aurally. ("Say no to the devil, say no!" – "Sejmou ti podobu sejmou!").[16]

15) In the Czech original the information is specified: "…jak to bylo řečeno příslušníky VB po koncertě v ZK ČKD Polovodiče Krč v Praze." The gig took place on 29th June 1972.
16) The quoted verse is translated here as follows: "They'll take down your appearance, yes they will." Svatopluk Karásek's texts translated into English were published in a booklet added to the record *Say No to the Devil*, Šafrán and Boží Mlýn, Uppsala, Sweden, 1979. [Vy silní ve víře / You who are Strong in the Faith, Kázání o svatbě v Káni galilejské / The Wedding in Cana, Podobenství o zrnu a koukolu / The Parable of the Good Seed and the Tares, Jak stromy volily krále / How the Trees Chose the King, Ženský sou fajn / Women are Wonderful, Kázání o zkáze Sodomy a Gomorry / The Destruction of Sodom and Gomorrah, Řekni ne ďáblu / Say No to the Devil, Já jsem ňákej stounavej / I Feel Old, Alone and Grey, Návštěva v pekle / a Visit to Hell,

The fact that Karásek as an evangelical pastor chooses religious themes for his songs is natural enough. But Charlie Soukup also has in his repertoire songs like *I Believe in God the Almighty* and *A Star is Rising*. In their song *Uncertainties*, the band Umělá Hmota sings: "On a mountaintop / pilgrims sat, / speaking quietly / of life and death". We have already described Zajíček of DG 307 as a chiliastic preacher. He says: "Each morning we should purify ourselves, / each evening we should make love. / Every second we should be / prepared for the end" – (*Purification*). "We have known much jollity / amidst the vanity / we have known poverty / so that we may fill our entity / this worldly sanctuary / is not our final destiny" – (*Our Friends*). "We're carriers of fear / We're prophets of dust" – (*The Way We Are*).[17] And in one of their recent songs, the Plastic People sing: "We live in Prague, / that is where / the Spirit Itself will / one day appear".[18]

Pavouci / Spiders, Je pozdě / It's too Late, Proroctví o příchodu Mesiáše / Prophecy on the Coming of the Messiah.] The quoted verse is translated here as follows: "They'll take down your appearance, yes they will."

17) On page 47 of the booklet/catalogue *The Merry Ghetto* there is a complete translation of this text which, however, bears the title *What Are We?*

18) From Egon Bondy's poem *Magical Nights*, whose complete translation was printed in the cover of the record *Egon Bondy's Happy Hearts Club Banned*. Another translation by Marek Tomin appears in the book *The Plastic People of the Universe* (Prague: Globus Music-Maťa, 1999). Yet another translation (and perhaps the best ever done so far) appears in the English subtitles of Jana Chytilová's documentary film *The Plastic People of the Universe* (2001): „Magical Nights of time's reign / Because of it Koch'll go insane / Magical Nights of time's reign // We live in Prague – that's the post / Where once'll appear the Holy Ghost / We live in Prague – that's the post" (from Bondy's collection of poems *Sbírečka*, 1974). The translation is by Jiří Popel. The editor cannot resist the temptation of quoting here one more of Popel's excellent translations of Bondy's poetry (from the same source). It is Bondy's poem *The Miraculous Mandarin / Podivuhodný mandarin*, one of the greatest hits of the PPU, an example of a pessimistic counterweight to *Magical Nights*, quoted by Jirous. Also this text was previously translated by P. Wilson (*MG*, 1978) and M. Tomin (*PPU*, 1999) – as *The Wondrous Mandarin*. Here it is in Popel's translation: "For your whole life you'll be spreading your legs to let in / The one and only Miraculous Mandarin // You'll be stitching your outfit from uselessness and sin / You'll keep searching for the Miraculous Mandarin // With a blood roar in your head and shadows in your grin / You'll keep longing for the Miraculous Mandarin // Many times you'll wish to gulp the gas like a gin / For again it wasn't the Miraculous Mandarin // When at the age of forty you'll hang down your chin / You'll know the Mills of God have sucked you in!"

I can understand why the establishment has little pleasure from all of this. But we too have little pleasure from the establishment. We have already mentioned that the way the audiences gather for concerts of all the groups mentioned here recalls the pilgrimages the Hussites were making into the mountains, with all their consequences. There is no point in enumerating the many concerts that were nipped in the bud, banned, or raided and broken up. It will be enough to mention the events around the concert in Rudolfov near České Budějovice on March 30, 1974, when police divisions attacked and beat up several hundred people who had come to the concert from all over the country. Chiliastic moods always arise in times when people begin to feel that the spiritual repression from the worldly powers is no longer bearable. It is natural that only some people feel this way, I am not talking about consumers. We are speaking about the people who live together in a mental ghetto that is not surrounded by walls, but it is scattered throughout an alien, unfriendly world.

This society which is based on spiritual kinship and mutual respect is in continual flux and it is continuously being reborn. The philosophical aspects of this stratum of people, or subculture, to use the jargon, was worked out in detail by Egon Bondy in his Utopian novel *The Invalid Siblings*.[19] The passages in which he describes the behaviour of the "invalids" – outcasts from consumer society – could be applied without modification to, for example, the First Music Festival of the Second Culture held in the small village of Postupice near Benešov.

Such a tightly knit but unorganized community of people would never have come into being had the pressure from the establishment not been so unbearable. It is a community for the mutual support of people who want to live differently, for whom the desire for mental and spiritual satisfaction stands higher on the scale of values than

---

(from Bondy's collection of poems *Pour Hélène la Belle – říkánky pro malé holky*, 1972).
19) Egon Bondy's chef d'oeuvre, the novel *Invalidní sourozenci*, has been published in the Czech original four times so far (Toronto: Sixty-Eight Publishers, 1981; Bratislava: Archa, 1991; Brno: "Zvláštní vydání...", 2002; Prague: Akropolis, 2012; it has been translated into Italian (*Fratelli invalidi*, Milan: Eleuthera, 1993), into German (*Die Invaliden Geschwister*, Heidelberg: Elfenbein, 1999), and into Slovenian (*Invalidna sorojenca*, Ljubljana: Police Dubove, 2017). In Martin Machovec's Seattle paper, 1997, the novel is mentioned as *The Disabled Siblings* (Machovec 2004).

the attempt to gain the material security offered to them by the establishment at the cost of repudiating everything that makes them a free being with a unique personality.

(XIII)
We must act with reason in this world of evil,
the place in which God has irrevocably placed us.[20]
JOHN MILTON

I have often used the term "underground" and twice the term "second culture". In conclusion, we should make clear what this is. In Bohemia, the underground is not tied to a definite artistic tendency or style, though in music, for example, it is expressed largely through rock music. The underground is a mental attitude of intellectuals and artists who consciously and critically determine their own stance towards the world in which they live. It is the declaration of a struggle against the establishment, the regime. It is a movement that works chiefly through the various art forms but whose representatives are aware that art is not and ought not to be the final aim of an artist's efforts. The underground is created by people who have understood that within the bounds of legality nothing can be changed, and who no longer even attempt to function within those bounds. Ed Sanders of the Fugs put it very clearly when he declared a total "attack on culture".[21] This attack can be carried out only by people who stand outside that culture.[22] Briefly put, the

20) See John Milton, *Areopagitica – A speech of Mr. John Milton for the Liberty of Unlicensed Printing, to the Parliament of England,* 1644; the original text: "To sequester out of the world into Atlantick and Eutopian polities, which never can be drawn into use, [we] will not mend our condition; but to ordain wisely as in this world of evill, in the midd'st whereof God hath plac'd us unavoidably."
21) Ed Sanders' slogan was first adopted in Czechoslovakia by Milan Knížák. See his song written in 1967 for the group Aktual, Atentát na kulturu [*The Assault upon Culture*]; in Milan Knížák, *Písně kapely Aktual,* Prague: Maťa, 2003.
22) See Ralf-Rainer Rygulla, his German epilogue to the bilingual anthology of American underground poetry *Fuck you! Underground Gedichte*; Darmstadt: Joseph Melzer Verlag, 1968; 2nd edition: Frankfurt/M.: Fischer Taschenbuch Verlag, 1968, p. 115: „Der von Ed Sanders geforderte »totale Angriff auf die Kultur« kann nicht durch

underground is the activity of artists and intellectuals whose work is unacceptable to the establishment and who, in this state of unacceptability, do not remain passive, but attempt through their work and attitudes to destroy the establishment. Two absolutely necessary characteristics of those who have chosen the underground as their spiritual home are rage and humility. Anyone lacking these qualities will not be able to live in the underground.

It is a sad and frequent phenomenon in the West, where, in the early 1960s, the idea of the underground was theoretically formulated and established as a movement, that some of those who gained recognition and fame in the underground came into contact with official culture (for our purposes, we call it the first culture), which enthusiastically accepted them and swallowed them up as it accepts and swallows up new cars, new fashions or anything else. In Bohemia, the situation is essentially different, and far better than in the West, because we live in an atmosphere of absolute agreement: the first culture doesn't want us and we don't want anything to do with the first culture. This eliminates a temptation that for everyone, even the strongest artist, is the seed of destruction: the desire for recognition, success, the winning of prizes and titles and last but not least, the material security which follows.

In the West many people who, because of their mentality, would perhaps belong among our friends, live in confusion. Here the lines of demarcation have been drawn clearly once and for all. Nothing that we do can possibly please the representatives of official culture because it cannot be used to create the impression that everything is in order. For things are not in order.

There has never existed a period in human history which could be considered an exclusively happy one; and genuine artists have always been those who have drawn attention to the fact that things are not in order. This is why one of the highest aims of art has always been the creation of unrest. The aim of the underground in the West is the destruction of the establishment. The aim of the underground here in Bohemia is the creation of a second culture: a

systemimmanente Kritik erfolgen, sondern durch Kritik von aussen, d. h. von Kriminellen, Süchtigen und Farbigen. [...] Die Leute vom Underground haben erkannt, dass innerhalb der Legalität nichts mehr verändert werden kann."

culture that will not be dependent on official channels of communication, social recognition, and the hierarchy of values laid down by the establishment; a culture which cannot have the destruction of the establishment as its aim because in doing so, it would drive itself into the establishment's embrace; a culture which helps those who wish to join it to rid themselves of the scepticism which says that nothing can be done and shows them that much can be done when those who make the culture desire little for themselves and much for others. This is the only way to live on in dignity through the years that are left to us and to all those who agree with the words of the Taborite chiliast Martin Húska who said: "A person who keeps the faith is more valuable than any sacrament".

Prague, February, 1975

[From *The Merry Ghetto*, a booklet/catalogue published with the record *Egon Bondy's Happy Hearts Club Banned*, Paris - London, 1978; translated from Czech by Paul Wilson and Ivan Hartel]

Paul Wilson
What's it Like Making
Rock'n'Roll in a Police State?

THE SAME AS ANYWHERE ELSE, ONLY HARDER.
MUCH HARDER

On a snowy day in March 1976, the phone rang in our flat in Prague. "Ahoy," said a familiar voice, a friend I've known since I first arrived in Prague back in 1967.[1] Like everyone else in the past couple of years, he didn't announce his name. It was a simple precaution in a time of growing paranoia.

"Ahoy," I replied. "What's happening?"

"They arrested the Plastic People and the whole Underground," he whispered.

"When?"

"Last night, this morning. It's still going on."

"Are you at home?"

"I'll be soon. I'm calling from a phone booth."

"I'll be right over."

I grabbed my coat and rushed down the wide staircase of the turn-of-the-century tenement house and into the street. As a former Plastic People band member and still an occasional participant, I had reason to fear I might also be rounded up. Thick, heavy snowflakes were drifting down, covering the ancient paving stones and the orange tiled roofs of Prague's Old Town. On the corner, boys were slapping a tennis ball against the wall of a Baroque church with hockey sticks. Here and there, forlorn graffiti stared out at me from the crumbling, rough-cast plaster that covers most buildings in the city: JETHRO TULL, BLACK SABBATH, a hammer and sickle joined to a swastika with an equal sign. I walked across the Charles Bridge, a medieval make-work project built six hundred years ago to span the Vltava River winding northward through the heart of Prague.

Less than two months ago, right here on this bridge, the Plastic People and about thirty other musicians had all posed for a picture to be used on the invitation to the Second Festival of the Second Culture, an underground event featuring twelve bands held in a secluded village tucked away in the South Bohemian hills.[2] Against

1) The author recalls that the then deliberately anonymous friend was Josef "Žluťák" Hrubý.

2) The village of Bojanovice where the so called Second Festival of the Second Culture took place in February 1976 is not actually situated in South Bohemia, but is just 25 km southwest of Prague.

all our expectations, the festival had not been raided by the police, and the triumph was still warming us, encouraging our hopes. Now the hunt was on again. The hopeful calm of the past two months had been nothing more than the eye of a hurricane. When I arrived in Czechoslovakia late in the summer of 1967 – to teach English and discover what Socialism was like in practice – the entire country was poised on the threshold of a tremendous political, social and cultural upheaval that has gone down in history as the Prague Spring.

One of the many signs of change in the air was rock'n'roll, or Big Beat, as the Czechs called it at the time. In 1967 and 1968, there were beat groups, beat clubs and beat festivals everywhere. In Prague alone there were hundreds of groups, ranging from neighborhood garage bands to professional groups with names like the Matadors, the Rebels, Juventus, Olympik, Flamengo, Vulkan or Stop the Gods.

By the standards I was used to, the concerts were not especially exciting, that is if you were looking for blazing, high-decibel, mind-searing performances. The bands tended to sound pedestrian and slack, and dancing when it was allowed at all, was Arthur Murray jive, but the young audiences were warm, and there was keen enthusiasm and eagerness in the air.

Contrary to what most people imagine, the Soviet invasion in August 1968 did not put a stop to things overnight. The momentum that was built up during the Prague Spring carried over well into 1969, and what ultimately killed it were not Russian tanks, but Czech bureaucrats.

It was in this immediate, post-invasion period in late 1968 that the Plastic People of the Universe – "The Psychedelic Band of Prague" – was formed. The moving spirit and founder of the group, bass player Milan Hlavsa, had come up through several bands with names like the Undertakers, the New Electric Potatoes and Hlavsa's Fiery Factory, before forming the Plastics with two of his schoolmates, Jiří Števich and Michal Jernek. Pavel Zeman, also from the neighborhood, filled out the lineup on drums. Eyewitness accounts of early Plastic People gigs all agree on one point: they made up in energy and showmanship for what they lacked in musical ability. In addition to Velvet Underground covers like *Venus In Furs* and Doors tunes like *Light My Fire* they were already playing their own material, wild compositions with suggestive titles like *Men Without*

Ears and *Crematorium Smoke* and incomprehensible lyrics. They wore strange costumes and garish makeup. The stage was banked high with huge speakers, only two or three of which worked. Their main prop was a large model flying saucer, and a big sign was fixed to the front of the podium, declaring in bold English: JIM MORRISON IS OUR FATHER!

This understandable defiance of biological paternity becomes even more meaningful when you realize that the Plastics, like most of their fans, had fathers who were in one way or another identified with the system. Števich's father was a secret policeman, Hlavsa's worked for the State Bank. Once Hlavsa had shot his brother in the stomach with an air rifle and then barricaded himself in his room with a hatchet when his brother and father had tried to force him to cut his hair. It took a psychiatrist to restore an uneasy truce to the family. Hlavsa's forearms were cross-hatched with scars. Flirtation with suicide, among some young Czechs, was an almost obligatory rite of passage.

In 1969, the Plastic People met Ivan Jirous. Jirous was a bright, energetic and very determined young man whose first loves were literature and art. Then he heard the Beatles. And, as the Lou Reed song goes, his life was changed by rock'n'roll. He came to Prague, studied art history, hung around the nascent rock scene, grew his curly chestnut hair long, and wrote inflammatory articles.

At the time, Jirous was working with the Primitives Group – who were a psychedelic band in Prague in those days – helping them to stage wild, extravagant shows that were more like happenings than rock concerts. But by the spring of 1969, he had begun to feel that the Primitives were stagnating, and when he saw the Plastic People play at the Beatsalon in 1969, he felt the old excitement all over again. They had, he said later, "that inner tension that has made rock into a spiritual instrument to set a whole generation in motion."

In a matter of weeks, Jirous had become the Plastics' artistic director, taking charge of everything except the business end of things – which at this stage was looked after by a professional manager – and the music, which he left in the band's hands.

In the fall of 1969, a friend introduced me to Ivan Jirous on the street and he invited us to come to his place for a potato dumpling feast, as he called it. At the time, he was living with his wife Věra in a small side street apartment in Prague's east end. Two of the Plastic People were already there when we arrived: Hlavsa, with long, sleek black hair, a spontaneous laugh and the features of a North American Indian, of which he was very proud; and Josef Janíček, a hard-working, soft-spoken fellow whose nose was slightly out of kilter. Janíček had recently joined the band after the Primitives (for whom he played guitar) split up.

During the long preparations for supper, in which everyone took part, Jirous kept up a running monologue on Czech history and on how, even in the blackest of times (and the times were steadily getting blacker now) the Czechs had always managed to keep the flame of culture alive. We drank vast quantities of lovely golden beer brought from the taproom across the street in large ceramic jugs. In between monologues, Jirous would put his favorite records on a battered turntable jacked into a World War II radio. Sated with heavy dumplings, sauerkraut and beer, I lay back and listened to the Velvet Underground, Captain Beefheart, the Doors and the Fugs, and as I listened, I began to feel a depth in the music that I had never felt before, as though I were hearing it for the first time with Czech ears. I remember in particular the Fugs' haunting, stripped down version of *Dover Beach* by Matthew Arnold. I'd studied the poem in school, but now the familiar lines, "And we are here as on a darkling plain... where ignorant armies clash by night" seemed to express directly the agony I knew so many Czechs were feeling, the agony of being caught in the middle of a pitched battle of faiths, ideologies and political systems, with no visible way out.

A few weeks later, in early December, I saw the Plastic People perform. It was at the steadiest gig they ever had, before or since, a weekly dance in a village called Horoměřice, just north of Prague. Every Sunday afternoon, three buses would collect all the long-haired kids from the beer halls of central Prague and drive them out to the village. The pub was a typical rural hostelry, with a taproom at one end and a large hall with a stage at the other. It was packed with kids, jostling one another around, smoking like furnaces and drinking beer as though they were afraid the pub-keeper would soon run out.

The stage was decorated with gigantic inflated polyethylene cigars.

Just as it was getting dark outside, the Plastics came on wearing white satin sheen gowns that looked as though they had slept in them, and dark, sinister makeup. When they broke into a spirited version of *White Light, White Heat*, half the audience rushed forward to the edge of the stage, while the other half broke into a loping, free-form dance that had nothing at all to do with Arthur Murray. At the climax of the song, a fellow with no eyelashes or eyebrows ignited two bengal fires, which filled the room with a choking, acrid smoke, then he squirted an ampoule of lighter fluid into his mouth and did a fire-breathing act right on the dance floor. The Plastics sang all the lyrics, even to their own songs, in English, though it wasn't an English I could understand. Their playing was rough and ragged at times, but I felt it only needed time to cure it. When Jirous loped over, rolling his eyes and shaking his hair, to ask what I thought, I told him they were wonderful, but that they needed to play together a lot more. He peered at me for a moment, and then said. "Have you any idea, man, just how difficult it is to get gigs right now?"

I didn't, but was soon to find out.

In the fall of 1970, I was invited to join the band as vocalist and rhythm guitarist, along with Jiří Kabeš, a viola player who had once played for a 60s rock'n'roll group called the Teenagers. By this time, as part of the general cultural purges going on across the country, the Plastics had lost their professional status and with it, their basic equipment, most of which had been loaned to them by the state-run booking agency. And two of the original members, Števich and Jernek, had quit.

The plan was to regroup, become as self-sufficient as possible (Janíček, who was a good electrician, was making a P.A. system, a simple mixing board and an amplifier) and to play as amateurs while trying to regain the all-important professional status. The biggest problem, apart from equipment and instruments, was the Catch-22 that faces all amateur rock bands in Eastern Europe – where to practice. Without official status, it is impossible to get rehearsal space, and without rehearsal space, it is difficult to become good enough to satisfy the juries who sit in judgment over every musical act in the country.

We solved the matter temporarily by practicing acoustically in the flats of accommodating relatives. Even this was difficult. There is a chronic shortage of housing in Czechoslovakia and it is not unusual to find three generations living on top of one another in a single two-room flat. Extending hospitality to a five-piece rock band, therefore, is not something lightly undertaken, Moreover, although we could learn the vocal and instrumental parts this way, we had no way of knowing how we would sound onstage, amplified; it was like trying to paint a huge, full-color mural by candlelight. A lot of our rehearsal time was spent polishing the cover tunes we were doing, and this meant spending hours listening over and over again to the same records. The problem was that no one had a stereo set, and it was often painfully difficult to decipher words and individual instrumental lines in mono.

In addition to cover tunes, of course, the Plastics had their own growing repertoire, a lot of it based on a strange cosmo-mythological blend of everyday detail and mystical speculation. A lot of the texts or ideas were fed to them by Jirous or his wife, and when a poem or an idea caught Hlavsa's fancy, he would brood on it and then come to rehearsal with the bass line and the structure worked out in detail, with parts for the other instruments merely roughed out. He knew from the start what he wanted the final result to sound like, but there was always room in the original scheme for the rest of us to invent. Understandably, the Plastics' music was – and still is today – very weighted toward the lower registers, somewhat ponderous and unmelodic, moving forward in deliberate sections, each with its own structure and mood. The influence of Zappa, the Velvet Underground and the Fugs, of course, can be traced in all this, sometimes quite specifically. But the powerful atmosphere the music generated – and still generates – comes straight from the band's own collective genius.

Our first concert was in fact our first full-fledged rehearsal as well. Suchá is about thirty kilometers north of Karlovy Vary (Karlsbad) and the local beat club was a low-ceilinged, jerry-built "cultural center" with a stage at one end and garish, hand-painted portraits of dead rock stars on the walls. Our name was scarcely legible on the posters, but across the sign, in huge print was the legend: 20 METERS FROM THE WOODS! I discovered later that this too had to do with the housing shortage in Czechoslovakia. Young lovers had almost no chance to be alone and rock concerts held near an accommodating forest were an ideal solution.

With Jimi Hendrix peering at us from the black wall, we set up and did a sound-check that we managed to drag out for almost an hour while we surreptitiously ran through as much of our repertoire as we could squeeze in. The manager, a thin, jittery fellow with a goatee, paced nervously up and down. He had a large crowd of teenagers milling around outside, drinking cheap vermouth and getting surlier by the minute. As soon as we finished, they surged into the hall.

We couldn't have asked for a better opening act, Aktual was a group put together by Czech artist Milan Knížák using very unconventional instruments (like power tools and Jawa motorcycles) played by a bunch of rootless kids plucked off the streets of Marienbad. They were far more audacious artistically and musically than we were, and the audience had come expecting something more conventional. Although we were still awkward and out of focus, we at least sounded more like what they were used to. Still, the concert was a shock to me. We had no monitors, neither then nor later, so I couldn't hear myself sing or play, and what I could hear sounded awful. There was a lot of coming and going in the audience, yet they seemed glad to have us there. Any rock'n'roll band was better than none.

During the two years I was with the Plastic People, we played about fifteen times, by my rough count, in front of a live audience. And that was the band's heyday. The type of concert varied. Sometimes it would be a simple high school or youth club dance. Sometimes it would be a special event like the Homage to Andy Warhol gig in February 1972 at the Music F Club in Prague, where Jirous gave a slide show and lecture on American pop art and we "illustrated" it with songs by the Velvet Underground. We played in small towns and large cities, and wherever we went, we were followed by a band of faithful fans who were always there when we played, regardless of weather or distance. We often left mixed reactions behind us – usually the split was along age lines – but people never forgot us.

One indication of the slow spread of the band's reputation – or notoriety – was the fact that the police were beginning to take an interest in what we were doing. Sometime in 1971 they began an investigation into whether we were making money illegally. ("Indulging in illegal enterprise" is how the criminal code phrases it.) One by one (myself excepted, for some reason) the Plastics were interrogated, but no charges were made.

In the fall of 1971, we finally found a place to rehearse that was not in someone's lap. It was an old brick vaulted cellar in a condemned tenement house in Holešovice, just a shift away from the Prague abattoirs. The dirt floor was littered with butts, broken glass and wires. There was no heat and when winter set in, we practiced in our coats and kept warm with bottled beer and rum. The only concession to beauty in the place was a Mothers of Invention poster stolen from a hoarding in Berlin. But it was a magic place, because for the first time since I joined the band, we could actually spend time playing together, and not just learning mechanical riffs to be glued together later onstage. It was at this point, I think, that what the Plastics had absorbed from the Velvet Underground and other groups started to loosen up their own more structured approach to songwriting: they began coming up with material that, of all their music, was the most clearly poised between America and Europe.

We premiered the new material above ground in June 1972 in a factory works club on the other side of Prague.[3] It was the largest concert we had ever played in the city, and also the last. Egon Bondy, an underground poet who was also very popular with the younger generation, was in the audience, and was ecstatic at what he heard. He remarked that the Plastics must try to put his poetry to music. And so the seed was planted, for out of the collaboration grew the music that eventually appeared on their first LP, *Egon Bondy's Happy Hearts Club Banned*.

That same evening, a drunken auxiliary police officer provoked a shoving incident in the lobby of the building. Two uniformed cops arrived and while Jirous was trying to explain the situation to them, they shot mace into his eyes from point-blank range and dragged him off to a local police station. He was released later that night after the whole thing had been explained by friends and witnesses

3) The gig in ZK ČKD Polovodiče, Krč, Prague, also mentioned by I. M. Jirous. It took place on 29th June 1972.

who went with him to the police station. But there were no more concerts in Prague and soon after that, the Plastics were forced to move out of the cellar. The tenement house in Holešovice was pulled down to make way for a vacant lot full of weeds.

When I left the band later in 1972, it was not a split but a gradual drifting away that had to do with the new direction they were moving in. As long as their music had primarily been based on Western rock music and sung in English, there was something I could bring to the band out of my own experience and background. But now the band was being pulled more powerfully back toward its own roots by a desire to address its audience in its own language and regardless of how far I had managed to assimilate, this was something I couldn't contribute to, though I supported the move entirely.

The basic shift in direction coincided with the arrival of saxophonist Vratislav Brabenec, a lanky redhead with a nose even further out of joint than Janíček's; Brabenec had a background in jazz rather than rock, and he could play soaring, exhilarating freeform solos that were apparently at odds with the more formalistic approach the Plastics had. Brabenec resolutely refused to have any truck with cover tunes, and the die was cast. In later 1972, with Brabenec aboard, the Plastics tried once again to gain professional status. This time, quite unexpectedly, a jury of official pop stars, music critics and other musicians were impressed enough to grant them a license. Two weeks later, however, a letter arrived from the Prague Cultural Center (PKS) – the booking agency – overturning the jury's decision on the grounds that the Plastics' music was "morbid" and would have a "negative social impact". Ivan Jirous immediately phoned PKS and asked them if there were any other agencies that could authorize the Plastics to perform in public. He was told that PKS was the only one. Thus began the strategy of creating private occasions to perform, like wedding celebrations or birthday parties. There could be no question of giving up or turning back.

As it became more and more difficult to do things "officially", the underground music scene in Prague began to grow, and there can be no doubt that the example set by Jirous and the Plastics was a major inspiration. A young poet, Pavel Zajíček, joined with Hlavsa to form a group called DG 307, essentially a voice band that used unconventional instrumentation to create dramatic nerve-lacerating settings for Zajíček's visionary verse. Another band formed in this period was a proto-punk outfit called Umělá Hmota (Artificial Material), which quickly divided like a living cell into two units. The UH bands were raw, energetic, and direct, learning as they performed, and their music owed as much to the Plastics as it did to American bands like MC 5. Already the underground was developing its own style and traditions.

At the same time, the sense of being encircled by hostile forces grew. In the summer of 1973, Ivan Jirous was arrested along with three friends after they insulted a pensioner in a Prague beer hall. Normally, they would have spent the night in the drunk tank and been released, but the pensioner was a retired secret policeman and the insult had included the phrase "bald-headed Bolshevik". All four were sent to prison, Jirous pulling ten months.

While he and the others were still in jail, the Plastics were asked to play at a concert near the city of České Budějovice in South Bohemia, an event that would come to be known as the Budějovice Massacre.[4] By now rock concerts were so rare that the news spread like a prairie fire, and hundreds of kids from all over the country converged on Budějovice for a serious good time. But before the Plastics had a chance to play, several busloads of police arrived, cancelled the event and then ordered everyone out of town. Masses of young people were herded into the Budějovice train station by cops and soldiers with dogs and riot gear, and were then driven through a tunnel leading under the tracks to the platforms. The tunnel was lined with truncheon-wielding goons, and a lot of blood was spilled and limbs broken. All those destined for Prague were crammed Nazi style into one end of a single passenger car and then, as the train rocked and rolled back to Prague, they were taken one by one into a compartment, photographed, interrogated briefly, and then sent to the other end of the car. At every station along the way, there were hoards of policemen making sure that no one escaped. In the end, six people were sent to prison and dozens were expelled from school. The Budějovice Massacre was a well-coordinated paramilitary operation, the opening skirmish in a holy war against unconventional rock music that has been going on ever since.

---

4) The event took place in Rudolfov, near České Budějovice, on 30ᵗʰ March 1974.

The response of the underground was typical: business (or pleasure) as usual. A few months later, in September 1974, the first large festival of underground music was held.[5] Smaller concerts were organized from time to time in towns near Prague. Despite the extreme discretion with which these events were planned the police almost always showed up. Sometimes they merely took the names of everyone there; at other times, they made arrests, but from the Budějovice Massacre on, the police were a constant factor in anything the underground did. That was why it was so astonishing when none showed up at the second festival of underground music in January 1976.[6] Now, as I found myself walking across the Charles Bridge two months later, watching the snow float down onto the venerable roof tops of Prague, it seemed clear to me that the police had used those two quiet months to prepare for their next big move.

Over a bottle of Myslivecká, a caustic, rye-based drink, my friend and I surveyed the devastation: twenty-seven people, most of them members of the Plastic People, DG 307, Umělá Hmota and Hever & Vazelína Band, arrested; the Plastics' amps, speakers and some instruments, most of it painstakingly constructed by hand over the past five years and shared out among the underground bands on a communal basis, seized; dozens of flats raided, ransacked and countless photos, tapes, samizdat texts and books confiscated; over a hundred people interrogated, it was the largest police action in the country since the early 70s, and, in an unexpected way, it changed the face of rock'n'roll in Czechoslovakia.

The very next day, the Western press agencies in Prague picked up the story and sent it out. The news caused ripples of consternation and incomprehension in the West: "The Czechs lock people up just for their music? Incredible!" Within twenty-four hours, the news was beaming back into Czechoslovakia via the BBC, the Voice of America and Radio Free Europe, which has an estimated three million listeners. Suddenly, the whole country knew about the Plastic People of the Universe. The government retaliated – too

5) The so-called First Music Festival of the Second Culture, held in the village of Postupice near Benešov on 1st September 1974.
6) The so-called Second Music Festival of the Second Culture, held in the village of Bojanovice, southwest of Prague, on 21st February 1976 (not in January!).

late – with its own gutter press version of the arrests: these so-called musicians and artists, said *Rudé Právo*, the Party daily, were just long-haired neurotic drug addicts and mental cases who took delight in the grossest of perversions and deliberately sang vulgar, antisocial songs. For the thousands of disaffected and alienated young people in the country, it was the best advertisement the Plastics could have wished for.

Another unexpected consequence of the arrests was that the banned intellectual elite of Czechoslovakia – people who had been ousted from public life after the Soviet invasion – rallied to the defense of the underground bands. A group of intellectuals, including the playwright Václav Havel and the philosopher Jan Patočka, wrote an open letter to West German novelist Heinrich Böll appealing for support. A former member of Dubček's politburo[7] wrote an open letter to the leaders of Czechoslovakia, and so did a group of ex-lawyers and ex-judges, themselves all victims of the political repression.

By the time the underground was brought to trial, all but seven had been released from prison. The rest were charged with an "organized disturbance of the peace". In one trial, three members of the band Hever & Vazelína were sentenced to up to fifteen months in prison. In the major trial, which took place in Prague in September 1976, Ivan Jirous, Vratislav Brabenec, Pavel Zajíček and Sváťa Karásek were sentenced to terms ranging from eight months to one and a half years. Jirous was given the longest.

Inspired by the example of the musical underground, and by the energy and solidarity the trials had generated, Václav Havel (now in prison himself) and others went on to give shape to the human rights movement launched in January 1977. The result was Charter 77, a manifesto calling for the Czechoslovak regime to honor the commitments to human rights that it made by signing the Helsinki Agreements and the UN covenants. While it lifted people's spirits tremendously, Charter 77 also brought the roof down. The police made widespread arrests and harassed the signatories endlessly, and this time I was picked up too, in a classic, early morning arrest.

---

7) A former member of Dubček's politburo: Zdeněk Mlynář, "Proti falši a lži. Otevřený dopis politickým činitelům, odpovědným za zákonnost v ČSSR," *Listy*, VI, no. 6 (Rome: December 1976, p. 5).

During the eight-hour interrogation that followed, I refused to talk about anyone but myself, but what I said was apparently enough.

I was given until July 15, 1977 to leave the country.

A few days before my departure, the Plastics and I got together, polished up all the songs we used to do together, and held a small party for about fifty people in an old house in the hills near Děčín in Northern Bohemia.[8] For a couple of hours we played the old repertoire, reliving the days that now seemed as distant as an idyllic dream of youth, the days when it was still possible to pretend, for a while at least, that we were living in a normal country.

At midnight, there was a knock on the door. Suddenly, the house was crawling with police and within half an hour, about ten of us were on our way down the winding road in the back of squad cars. In Děčín the police station was bustling with red-eyed plainclothesmen carrying truncheons. I was separated off from the rest and when I refused to be interrogated, they put me in a car and drove me back toward Prague. As we got close to the city where I had spent almost ten years of my life, the cop beside me in the back seat – who I learned later may have been Koudelka, the mastermind of the whole police campaign against the underground – said to me:

"Look, you'll be leaving the country in a few days. When you get to the West, we don't want you doing anything – you know – to help the Plastics. Know what I mean?"

"When I get to the West, I'll be outside your jurisdiction."

"Is your wife going with you?"

"She hasn't got her papers yet."

"But I take it you want to see her again."

I looked at him, but I couldn't see his face in the dark.

"Call it blackmail if you want," he said, "but you'd better believe me." The driver pulled the car over to the side of the road and stopped. We were still in the middle of empty, black countryside. "Our orders were to take you to Prague," Koudelka said. "Here you are."

He pointed up ahead. A small dirty sign leaned crazily over the ditch, PRAHA. The driver got out and opened my door, which had no handle on the inside.

---

8) The farewell party and concert was held in Jan Princ's family house in the village of Rychnov, near Děčín, on 9th July 1977.

"Goodbye, Mr. Wilson. And if I were you, I'd advise your friends to lay off the music-making for a while."

"If you can't stop them, how can I?"

The door slammed, the car spun around and I was left standing there in the night with the lights of Prague flickering faintly in the distance like a constellation of fallen stars.

A few days later, I arrived in London, England to wait for my wife to come out. It was the summer of 1977 and punk rock was in full swing, joyful exuberance in grimy clubs, mindless weekend punch-ups on Sloane Square, instant analysis in the *New Society*. The same bands that the Plastic People had been inspired by ten years ago – The Velvets, Captain Beefheart – were now being redis- covered. I went to an early Slits/Sham 69 gig where the new Sex Pistols documentary was shown, full of arrests, protest, rage and *lese-majesté*. Afterward I approached someone in the Pistols' en- tourage with a suggestion: why not smuggle a copy of the film into Czechoslovakia, give the Plastic People a lift.

"The Plastic People?" he responded in a dead-eyed, cocky public school whine. "They're anti-socialist. I don't support fascist rock bands. I'd rather send the film to South Africa."

Ah yes, images of Sid Vicious smelling his socks to raise con- sciousness in Soweto. I was sorry I'd asked.

Back in Czechoslovakia, Ivan Jirous was released from prison in the fall of 1977 and almost immediately rearrested after making some inappropriate remarks at the opening of an art exhibition.[9] He got another eighteen months. Then last November he was arrested a fourth time – this time for his connection with an underground magazine called *Window*.[10]

In September of this year, his sentence of three and a half years in a maximum security prison was upheld by an appeals court. In such prisons, you are allowed a single one-hour visit per year. Most

9) I. M. Jirous was arrested and imprisoned for the third time in October 1977. The pretext was his speech at the opening of an art exhibition (Jiří Lacina's) in Prague. He spent 18 months in prison.

10) I. M. Jirous was arrested and imprisoned for the fourth time in November 1981 – al- legedly for helping publish the samizdat magazine *Vokno* (*Window*). He spent 3 and a half years in prison where he wrote his chef d'oeuvre, a collection of poems *Magorovy labutí písně* (*Magor's Swan Songs*).

of your fellow inmates are lifers. There are serious fears that Jirous will not survive. It is a heavy price to pay for keeping the faith, ignited long ago by a few Anglo-American rock bands.

The Plastic People continued to write music, but they were, and still are, constantly harassed by the police. Younger bands tend to avoid them, says Vratislav Brabenec, who has been living in Vienna since last April, because they carry the police around with them like lice. Still, since 1977, they have managed to write, record and perform four major works. Outstanding among them is the *Passion Play*, a magnificent rock rendition of the Crucifixion of Christ. It was performed and recorded in a barn belonging to Václav Havel while the barn was surrounded by platoons of police, staked out in the fields and woods around the farm. The Plastics have also performed in country houses, but in every case, the police have subsequently either blown the place up or burned it down. Their most recent work, a cycle of songs based on the work of the radical Czech philosopher Ladislav Klíma, and a concert based on lyrics by Vratislav Brabenec can scarcely be described in musical terms any more.[11] They are the distillation of a struggle. On the surface, it's a struggle with a regime that cannot tolerate any music or art except that made in its own image. But essentially, it is a struggle between the principles of life and death.

A new generation is coming up in the Czech underground, however, and there are signs that, despite the repression, the scene is spunky and alive. A year ago, over thirty groups were banned in Prague alone, a fact that is more hopeful than it first appears. The new bands have names like Energie G, Garage, Frogs' Phlegm and Dog Soldiers.

A decade ago, the Plastic People stood almost alone. Now their progeny carry on. Even officially sanctioned music magazines reflect the fact that rock'n'roll is on the boil in Czechoslovakia. Yet the

---

11) The concert given by the Plastic People in October 1979 – *Jak bude po smrti* (*How It Will Be After Death* or *Afterlife*) – with music based on texts by Ladislav Klíma, took place in an underground community country house in the village of Nová Víska, near the towns of Kadaň and Chomutov, Northern Bohemia. The recording was last released on the CD: The Plastic People of the Universe, *Jak bude po smrti, PPU VI, 1979*, (Praha: Globus International, 1998).

band that kept the flame alive through the 70s is never mentioned in print. Officially, the Plastic People do not exist.

Recently Milan Hlavsa was waiting for a light to change and overheard a conversation between two Prague teenagers.

"Have you heard? The Plastics are all in America."

"Bullshit, man," said the other. "They're all in jail."

And Hlavsa, his ghostly non-persona smiling, brushed intangible shoulders with them and walked on by.

February 1983
[*Musician* magazine]

Egon Bondy
The Roots of the Czech Literary Underground in 1949–1953

The Czechoslovak underground of the 1970s and the 1980s was an important component of the unofficial culture, and inside this context it comprised many elements of the counterculture. In comparison with other countries of the Eastern Bloc, it has been much more artistically productive, from rock'n'roll to the visual arts.[1] Within the realm of the Czech underground, there existed projects such as a 14-volume history of world philosophy,[2] an undertaking that took place simply because no such publication has been available for more than 40 years.

Czech underground translation projects have also been extensive. New periodicals have appeared, comparable in coverage to journals published abroad. The underground culture, influencing large numbers of participants, has not been limited to major population centres or intellectual circles, but attracted enough attention, particularly among working youth. The rapid growth of the counterculture in 1972–1973 was facilitated, in part, by works created 20 years earlier. The younger generation discovered them, reproduced them, presented them, wrote music to them, and found inspiration in them. The roots of the Czechoslovak underground therefore reach as far back as 1949–1953, the period in which the underground had not yet been conceived. The purpose of this paper is to show that these early works can be, perhaps uniquely inside the Eastern Bloc perceived as the building blocks of the contemporary underground movement.

It must be noted that Czech art between the two world wars played a much more important role in the international modern art scene than the art of any other Central or Eastern European country. After the rise of Fascism in Germany, Prague was second only to Paris as the most important center of moden art. Czech underground culture grew from this modernist tradition, particularly its surrealist past.

---

1) A typical example of Czech underground myth: evidence of an almost complete absence of contacts among unofficial art and literary circles in different countries of the Soviet Bloc.

2) The author refers to his own work which he initiated in 1977 and finished only at the beginning of the 1990s. His work was divided into 14 samizdat volumes, but between 1991–1996 it was published in 6 regular books. (*Poznámky k dějinám filosofie I.-VI.*, Prague: Vokno, 1991–1996.)

In 1950, several young members of the Czechoslovak Surrealist Group, which had been already illegal by then, broke away from their predecessors because they felt that the established surrealist aesthetic was no longer capable of reflecting the world into which they were thrust. As I will show, this was not merely an academic point of disagreement but a matter of life-style and "Weltanschauung". Initially, the runaway group was relatively large – most of us were about twenty years old. However, with the passage of time, only several people remained actively involved – namely Honza Krejcarová, Ivo Vodseďálek, Egon Bondy, and Vladimír Boudník.[3] In the years 1951–1954, we also included Bohumil Hrabal, our senior by a generation. From 1949 to 1954 we had published in a samizdat edition, "Midnight" (Půlnoc), 34 smaller and larger volumes.[4] The works of the group's prominent members met various fates.

Honza Krejcarová, daughter of Milena Jesenská, was most severely affected by the raids of the secret police. What remains of her work is only a small corpus of poems in the then absolutely unique "hard sex" style, a collection of the so-called *Poems from Therapy* based on the use of psychoanalytical symbolism, and short erotic prose.[5] During the 1960s, Krejcarová officially published commercial literature in order to make a living.

Ivo Vodseďálek wrote, with some pauses, all his life and remained most faithful to the original theoretical and aesthetic principles of the group. After 1953, he refused to publish even in the samizdat

3) Only Egon Bondy (Zbyněk Fišer) and Jana "Honza" Krejcarová-Černá were in contact with the Czechoslovak Surrealist Group of Karel Teige and Vratislav Effenberger; see the samizdat anthology *Židovská jména* [Jewish Names], 1949 (published only in 1995, Prague: NLN).

4) According to a more recent estimation, the Půlnoc edition numbered some 44 samizdat volumes (see Martin Machovec, "Několik poznámek k podzemní ediční řadě PŮLNOC", *Kritický sborník*, XIII, 3, 1993), or even 48 (see Egon Bondy, "2000"; Martin Machovec, "Ediční poznámka," both in *Revolver Revue* 45, 2001).

5) The "hard-sex" style: a collection *V zahrádce otce mého* [*Dans les jardins d'mon père*], 1948; *Poems from Therapy* (*Therapeutické texty* [*básně z therapie*]): one of the volumes of the Půlnoc edition which has not been found yet and is known only from samizdat bibliographies; the short erotic prose mentioned by the author, *Clarissa*, was published in a single volume with other early texts by Krejcarová, *Clarissa a jiné texty*, Prague: Concordia, 1990. All Krejcarová-Černá's texts were published again in *Tohle je skutečnost (Básně, prózy, dopisy)*, Prague: Torst, 2016.

form because he had not been satisfied with his works. He finally made them available in summer 1989. When his collected works are published in the near future, the history of the last forty years of Czech literature will require substantial correction, I can assure you.[6]

Egon Bondy is a relatively fruitful writer of poems and novels who also assisted with the rebirth of the underground movement in the 1970s. As a result, his works are well known among today's Czechoslovak youth.[7]

In contrast to Bohumil Hrabal, all three authors categorically refused to publish excerpts of their work during the 1960s as well as during the following decades. It is worth noting that only Bondy had political reasons for it, since his writing is rather explicit in this respect.

What did we come up with and what did we do then? Claiming that after the Communist takeover in February 1948, we suddenly found ourselves living in an Orwellian world is a commonplace. Moreover, our shock had been amplified by the pervasive Stalinist propaganda: the metropolis had been plastered all over with posters in the Socialist Realist style, featuring linguistically and conceptually absurd slogans. The fact that other media – the press, film and radio broadcasting – produced similar results is worth mentioning only to complete the picture. It was impossible to resist this attack and most people could not resist it because it was a completely unexpected and unprecedented situation, even for those having experienced Nazi propaganda. Its effects did not take long to materialize. Enthusiasm for Stalinism became widespread, particularly amongst the young in the years 1948–1954. For instance, many of my

---

6) Ivo Vodseďálek's poetical works of 1949-1989 have been published in five volumes as *Dílo Ivo Vodseďálka 1-5* (Prague: Pražská imaginace, 1992).

7) Egon Bondy's poetical works of 1950-1988 were published in nine volumes as *Básnické dílo Egona Bondyho I-IX* (Prague: Pražská imaginace, 1990-1993). See also some of his texts translated into English in *The Plastic People of the Universe* [English edition of texts put into music], Praha: Globus Music-Maťa, 1999; some more poems by Bondy translated into English & an extract from his novel *Sklepní práce* [Cellar Work] were published in: *Yazzyk Magazine* 1, Prague, 1992. Recently a critical edition, with commentary, of all of his poetic works has been published in three volumes: *Básnické spisy I-III*, (Prague: Argo, 2014, 2015, 2016).

colleagues who are present here at our conference spent this time actively contributing to and participating in Stalinist politics and propaganda. They will undoubtedly remember how often the hysterical deification of Stalin and of his socialist development programme reached the levels of paroxysm – when masses of Young Builders of Socialism were not only collectively cheering, singing, dancing and constructing, but they also collectively cried, condemned, hated, etc. I believe that they were not aware of the hidden side of that period – mass arrests and rapidly expanding concentration camps – although political trials and executions had the widest possible publicity for propaganda purposes. In any case, for us, the young poets and artists, this situation demanded that we offer an artistic response to what was happening around us, an offensive response. Thank God that we were too young to choose internal exile.

What we had arrived at was the aesthetic theory of the so-called *poetry of embarrassment* (*trapná poesie*) and *total realism* (*totální realismus*): embarrassing in the innermost sense of the word and total in a profoundly ambivalent sense of the word. We discovered and realized the possibility of using the pseudo-aesthetics of Stalinist mythology for its very refutation. We did not resort to irony or to anti-propaganda. For instance, we took advantage of the Stalinist slogans, giving it a unique aesthetic meaning which was reminiscent to some extent of Duchamp's treatment of his ready-mades. We neither underestimated nor doubted the emotional charge of the Stalinist artistic production: we amplified it to the very verge of vertigo and *ad absurdum*. Our poems from that period were sometimes constructed as seemingly naive, apparently unsuccessful attempts to emulate Stalinist aesthetics – with a clumsy use of meter or rhyme or a "misfit" metaphor that is not ironic but merely embarrassing. Sometimes these poems were written as a simple cut from some report or they gathered reality into a laconic total expression – within the length of six or seven verses, there was a simple statement about how we make love while the public system loudspeakers were almost simultaneously broadcasting news about the executions and reporting the exact time.[8] We strictly excluded from our poetics not

8) Egon Bondy's poems from the collection *Totální realismus*, 1950: "Tlampače na ulicích oznamují přesný čas / hodiny v nichž se vypíná elektřina / výsledky nejnově-

only didactics and moralizing, but also humor ("esprit") and any final point. We intentionally and successfully resisted both.

Indeed, it is difficult to document such statements without any relevant written material. I have no time for it in my presentation, still, I managed to bring samizdat literature from that period, thus it will be possible during the conference to arrange for impromptu translations of some parts. Let me at least quote from the memoir of Ivo Vodseďálek:

"We saw the gigantic Soviet perspectives of joy and pride in their artworks. They were not «reflections of reality», as some art historians tried to tell us. They formed the unique system of complex mythology that could establish moral and aesthetic values (...) Once faced with these works, our past ideals seemed compromised and undesirable. We began to understand reasons for generally missing the need for freedom that had until then stood at the summit of the hierarchy of values. It was quite an absurd situation, indeed."[9]

Our style had been naturally progressing over the course of time. From the very beginning extensive works were also created, whether they took the form of novellas or epic poetry. For the history of the Czechoslovak underground it is important as well as symptomatic that at the beginning of the 1970s its young writers reached directly for literature that we produced in 1949–1953 and adopted it as their own. From then on, these literary works and their specific poetics influenced the young generation to such an extent that some younger poets working during the 1980s (Jan Placák, Petr Placák, Jáchym Topol, Krchovský, and others) used to be called, in a would-be derisive way, the Bondy generation.

---

jších procesů / a sportovních utkání" ("The street loudspeakers announce the exact time / the hours when electricity is switched off / the results of the latest trials / and of the sport matches"); "Četl jsem právě zprávu o procesu s velezrádci / když jsi přišla / Po chvíli jsi se svlékla / a když jsem si k tobě lehl / byla jsi jako vždy příjemná // Když jsi odešla / dočetl jsem zprávu o jejich popravě" ("I was just reading report about the trial of the traitors / when you came / After a while you undressed / and I lay down beside you / and you were kind to me as usual // When you left / I finished reading report about them being executed").

9) From Vodseďálek's essay "Urbondy", see Ivo Vodseďálek, *Felixír života* (Brno: Host, 2000, p. 19).

At this moment I would like to point out what is in fact most interesting and most important from the vantage point of comparative literature. Some remarkable developments, which took place among members of the group that had published the edition "Midnight" in 1949–1953, were undoubtedly results of the fact that Czech art had, as I said, kept apace with the developments in international modern art. It is evident that there was an almost direct analogy to the literature of the American Beat Generation – which we preceded by several years – and that there were other apparently and clearly anticipated developing trends toward pop-art and hyper-realism.

I am not by any means interested in making some declaration based on particular chronological priority. I wish only to stress synchronicity in development, given on the Czech side by the vital character of modern art. The authors of the "Midnight" edition lived their lives in an environment that was more cruel and dangerous than was the milieu we have learned about from the biographies and the works of the Beat Generation. Under an incessant cloud of war, in the shade of forced labor camps and the mass political persecution, our way of life developed certain analogies with the Beats, such as be-bop (strictly forbidden and punished, of course), hard sex (with the exclusion of homosexuality),[10] vagabondage, begging, theft (we stole everything but cars, which were not around at that time), and anti-social activities of any kind. We became the vagrants and the homeless, and, in line with the political situation of that period, the exiles in the most literal sense of the word. At the time of forced employment (it was illegal to be unemployed), we refused to work and, as a consequence, we could not obtain food vouchers to exchange for food. At the time of complete control of all the citizens through files and written records, we had no work registration cards and no personal identity documents. We were drinking fruit vermouth instead of taking drugs and, instead of cruising across the United States, we used to cross the state border back and forth under fire,

10) This claim should be taken with some reservation. There are testimonies (Hrabal, Boudník, Krejcarová, Herda) suggesting that homosexuality was not alien to at least some of the members of the Půlnoc edition circle.

in order to smuggle in some nylon stockings from Austria.[11] Instead of Zen Buddhism, we had Ladislav Klíma, a paramystical Czech philosopher from the beginning of the twentieth century (who will be also discussed at this conference) and Leon Trotsky.

All this was an expression and a mode of instinctive defense against the totalitarian establishment. This was naturally accompanied by a corresponding life style, one that we openly expressed in our work just as our American counterparts did in *Howl* or *On the Road*. The texts themselves stand as powerful evidence of this. The period I am referring to started in 1949 and finished with the year 1952. The last passages of Egon Bondy's epos *Remnants of an Epic* (*Zbytky eposu*) were written in 1954; by now the lost prose which at that time excited Hrabal was written in 1952–1953; the retrospective *Cadre Questionnaire* (*Kádrový dotazník*) in 1961.[12] In comparison, *Howl* appeared in 1953[13] and *On the Road* in 1957.[14] Living as we did, our experiences were comparably as intense as those of the Beats in the USA and we became a part of the dark side of official reality about which the up and coming literati from the state literary journals knew practically nothing.

We did not keep any contacts with these neophytes either in that period – when those who knew our activities called us "wreckers" and informed the police about us – or in the subsequent decades during which their opinions underwent several changes. We never tried to make any contact with the older generation of Czech poets (Seifert, Hrubín, Holan, et al.). The anti-authoritarianism on which we based our revolt was accompanied by anti-elitism at the

---

11) For more information about the author's experiences as a smuggler during the early 1950s, see his Czech memoirs *Prvních deset let*, (Prague: Maťa, 2002). The author's words "under fire" are to be considered a typical example of poetic license.

12) Author's error; the poem *Kádrový dotazník* was started in 1962 and was finished in 1967.

13) Author's error; correct date: 1956 (Ginsberg's *Howl* was first read in public in Six Gallery, San Francisco, 1955).

14) The year of the first publication of Kerouac's *On the Road* is correct, nevertheless it is worth noting that the book was written as early as 1951 and it was known in typescript at least to Kerouac's friends. Bondy's samizdat poems from the 1950s were known to his friends soon after they had been written.

intellectual level. The underground movement of the 1970s followed a similar path.

I will not discuss the analogy between the "Midnight" group and the Beat Generation any further because what we wrote then speaks for itself. I will rather turn to the second subject of my presentation. The aesthetics of poetry of embarrassment and of total realism anticipated the aesthetics and artistic creativity of pop-art and hyperrealism. We achieved, in theory as well as in practice, the point when banality as an aesthetic category begins to overlap with bestiality[15] as an aesthetic category – with the categories of the absurd and the scurrilous standing in between. The aggression of the trivial that keeps attacking us by picture and by word from commercial advertisements and from consumer goods was aesthetically exploited by pop-art. In a similar manner, we employed the aggression of the trivial which in Czechoslovakia of 1949–1953 consisted of omnipresent Stalinist fetish and slogans. (Quoting Vodseďálek: "Perhaps it is through this that a road leads away from Breton's fitfulness.[16] We felt this phenomenon in all realms of life, in politics, in sex and in art. Our goal was to glorify embarrassment. We had no idea how our program would be fulfilled by television broadcasting.")[17]

The moments of the mythological that are contained in the spellbinding quality of consumer symbols and their dream heroes were well known to us through analogical example of the political manipulation of consciousness. We typified this phenomenon, from the level of photographic documentation to the level of the most banal and most widespread consumer goods and used this method consciously. (Such a photographic document was, for instance, an unending row of politicians' portraits on a poster wall or a picture of salami often appearing on posters in a fetishist sense.) It is worth briefly mentioning that we recommended to the painter Mikuláš Medek, when he found himself on the verge of departing from surrealism, to try to paint an ordinary streetcar (no matter whether in

15) The expression "zrůdnost" is found in Czech original: the English translation could be "monstrosity" or "deformity".
16) The expression "křečovitost" is found in Czech original: from French "convulsive", therefore in English it might be "convulsive beauty".
17) From Vodseďálek's essay "Urbondy"; see note 9.

a veristic or naivist style) and simply write "Streetcar" under it, and so on. To Medek it seemed unacceptable and so he chose a road to abstraction.

To sum up, let me say only this: the roots of the Czechoslovak underground reach as far as the edition "Midnight" from the years 1949-1953, in the same sense that the roots of the American underground reach as far as the generation of the Beats. Some representatives of the "Midnight" group were – like the author of *Howl* in the U. S. – personally present at the beginnings of an "official" formation of the underground in Czechoslovakia. This tie across generations has been kept alive by both sides despite the fact that, for instance, Egon Bondy is generally known as a leftist Marxist. Typical of the Czechoslovak underground is its everpresent philosophical subtext (as evident in the works of Andrej Stankovič, Jan Placák, Jáchym Topol, and Fanda Pánek, the poet who writes without the benefit of any formal education) and a unique integration of harsh reality with a lyric dream – a late bequest of its surrealist grandparents. Both make the Czech underground attractive to a large readership and help it to penetrate the widest circles of youth. The history of the Czechoslovak underground is by no means at its end: it goes on despite the changes of the establishment.

Prague-New York 1990

Ivan Martin Jirous
On Czech Underground
Literature of the 70s and 80s

I am not a literary theoretician or a critic, and if some have regarded me in recent years as a poet, it is more by chance – I myself know that to be a poet is a much deeper vocation than just to have the skill to write something that resembles poems. By profession I am an art historian, but over the past twenty years I have not done much in this area. My only qualification to talk about the emergence of underground literature in the Czech lands is the fact that I was part of it almost from its very birth. From today's point of view – now that we can look back on an enormous number of samizdat periodicals and an immense quantity of ephemeral typescripts, the entire spectrum of underground literature is almost impossible to encompass and the story how it all began might sound almost improbable – the moment when a certain section of Czech literature was not so much created as consciously designated as "underground". We borrowed the term "underground" from the United States of America and applied it to the Czech situation – and some people still criticise us for doing so. Nevertheless, it seemed to us to be the best expression of the difference between official art and what we were aiming for. The use of the literal Czech translation *podzemí*, which denotes illegal or clandestine activity, would have been suicidal at a moment when the totalitarianism of the post-August era was at its worst.[1] In any case, over the past twenty years, both the word and the term underground have become a viable part of Czech culture. The term was spontaneously accepted mainly by people on the fringes of society. As a result it often became restricted to the cultural fringes made up of unsociable misfits and drop-outs, not to mention the fact they were incapable of creating works that would stand any real chance of success outside the narrow confines of the underground.

The dispute about what actually is and is not underground, who belongs to it and who does not, has been going on since the beginning of the period of "Consolidation", when it emerged in the Czech lands for the first time. I am not going to try to settle the controversy now; I simply want to draw attention to the sociological shift that occurred during the 70's and 80's.

1) By post-August era the author means the years following the Soviet invasion of Czechoslovakia in August 1968: the years of so-called "Normalization" or "Consolidation" in fact re-established the pro-Kremlin Brezhnev hard-liners; the period of totalitarian neo-Stalinism.

At the beginning of the 1970's the term was used exclusively in connection with rock music, particularly by people associated with the rock group The Plastic People of the Universe. In this connection it is necessary to point out that the soil nurturing this as well as many subsequent bands such as DG 307, Umělá hmota[2] and Bílé světlo[3] was quite different from the recent environment of rock underground culture. In the early 1970s people in the underground really had a working-class background and many of them were young vagrants. What we called underground expressed their instinctive rebellion and their attempt to live in a different way to what they saw around them in the greyness of "normalization" that began to overwhelm the colourful fragments of freedom which were glimpsed in the late 60s. Yet, the number of intellectuals who understood the spiritual and ethical potential of underground rock culture in those days could be counted on the fingers of one hand.

Be patient: I know I am supposed to be speaking about literature. But one cannot speak about the underground literature in the Czech lands without reference to the environment from which it began to spread. Underground rock music, particularly the music of the Plastic People, formed the nucleus of the expanding underground community from which literature emerged only subsequently.

This is not to say that literature was something unknown in the underground environment. Obviously it was being read and poems were set to music. But the fact that someone was a writer was often kept in secret inside the underground circles of those days. In an environment where rock music was the normal form of expression, poets considered their activity as something private and often even their closest circle of friends did not know they were writers. The incontrovertible breakthrough in this situation was the collection of poetry *Invalidní sourozenci Egonu Bondymu k 45. narozeninám* (*The Disabled Siblings for Egon Bondy on his 45th Birthday*), copied out in typescript in 1975. I edited it with Jiří Němec – and our biggest task was to discover who was writing anything within the underground circle. The collection included poetry and lyrics, some of them of

2) The name of the group is translated as *Artificial Matter*, *Artificial Material*, or *Synthetic Material*.
3) The name means *White Light* in English.

an ephemeral nature. For the first time a broader audience had access to texts by Vratislav Brabenec – known as the saxophonist of the Plastic People – Věra Jirousová, Andrej Stankovič, Fanda Pánek and Josef Vondruška,[4] to name only the poets whose fate was subsequently bound up with that of the underground. Another great poet included in the anthology – the graphic artist Naďa Plíšková[5] – essentially belonged to a different cultural circle.

It may sound unbelievable today but, at the time, the anthology shocked samizdat readers. Its impact on subsequent underground output – of whatever quality it may be – is undeniable. Other anthologies which followed were usually marking the 45th birthday of somebody in the underground. Underground literature, primarily poetry, began to appear in a variety of typewritten editions. After the first samizdat magazine *Vokno* (Window)[6] was founded in 1979, it regularly featured on its pages.

---

4) Vratislav Brabenec's poetical works of 1966 –1987 have been published in three volumes: *Sebedudy* (Prague: Vokno, 1992); *Karlín-Přístav*, (Prague: Maťa, 1995); *Sebedudy a jiné texty z let 1966-1987* (Prague: Kalich, 2010); see also some of his texts translated into English in *The Plastic People of the Universe* [English edition of texts put into music] (Prague: Globus Music–Maťa, 1999). Věra Jirousová's poetical works of 1964-1994 have been published in two volumes: *Co je tu, co tu není*, (Prague: Torst, 1995); *Krajina před bouří*, (Prague: NLN, 1998). Andrej Stankovič's, poetical works of the 60s, 70s, 80s, 90s have been published in four volumes: *Osvobozený Babylon – Slovenský Raj*, (Prague: Inverze, 1992); *Variace / Kecybely / Elegie / Nikdycinky*, (Brno: Host, 1993); *Noční zvuk pionýrské trubky – Patagonie* (Prague: Trigon, 1994); *To by tak hrálo, aby nepřestalo*, (Brno: Petrov, 1995). Fanda Pánek's poetical works of 1972-1990 have been published in three volumes: *Dnů římských se bez cíle plavíte*, (Praha: Vokno, 1993); *A tak za polární noci*, (Prague: Inverze, 1994); *Vita horribilis* (Prague: Kalich, 2007). Josef Vondruška's poetical works of 1975-1979 have been published in one volume *Rock'n'rollový sebevrah*, "Zvláštní vydání…" (Brno 1993). See also Vondruška's memoirs *Chlastej a modli se* (Prague: Torst, 2006).

5) Naďa Plíšková's poetical works of the 70s, 80s, 90s have been published in three volumes: *Plíšková podle abecedy*, (Prague: Dandy Club, 1991; *Hospodská romantika*, (Brno, Petrov, 1998); *Plíšková sobě*, (Prague: Torst, 2000).

6) The designation "the first samizdat magazine *Vokno*" should be understood as "the first *underground* samizdat magazine" since there were more samizdat periodicals founded before *Vokno*, issued by dissident groups and individuals who had nothing in common with the underground community of the Plastic People and their fans; see the quoted works by Posset and Prečan (see p. 81).

Let us return to the poets of the first anthology. We must also include Egon Bondy who precedes them by two generations but whose work during the seventies began to have an impact on the underground public – also thanks to the Plastic People who set Bondy's poems to music. Its impact was incomparably greater than in previous decades, when Bondy's work was known only to a handful of literary experts.[7] Through Bondy – and his camp followers of the 50s, i.e. Karel Hynek[8] and Honza Krejcarová[9] – the origins of underground poetry might be traced far back in the Communist past of the country. It was not however called underground then and, during the 1960s, particularly towards the end of the decade, a false impression shortly emerged, according to which there would be no need for underground literature to be created in the Czech lands. Today we know that it was only an impression and that the jubilation of the Prague Spring concealed the fact, for example, that the work by poet Egon Bondy was not published even then. The issue of *Tvář* magazine in which he could at least enjoy the proofread versions of his texts was never published.

After their mass distribution[10] in the 70s, Bondy's texts had probably the greatest impact on the rising underground generation – he shared this influence with Pavel Zajíček,[11] who disseminated his appellative messianic texts through DG 307, a sister band of the Plastic People. Moreover, a whole lot of imitations started to be written. People with no education wrote what they considered to be poetry.

7) For more information about the editions of Bondy's poetical works, see note 7 to his essay published in this volume.

8) Karel Hynek's poetical works have been published in one volume: *S vyloučením veřejnosti*, (Prague: Torst, 1998).

9) About the editions of Krejcarová's poetical works see note 5 to Bondy's essay published in this volume.

10) By "mass production" the author means the mass samizdat dissemination and distribution of texts.

11) Pavel Zajíček's poetical works of the 70s have been published in two volumes: *DG 307: Texty z let 1973-1980* (Prague: Vokno, 1990); *Zápisky z podzemí: 1973-1980* (Prague: Torst, 2002). Some of Zajíček's lyrics translated into English appear in the booklet *The Merry Ghetto*, in the book *The Plastic People of the Universe* [texts of songs] (1999), and in the leaflet added to the record *DG 307: gift to the shadows (fragment)*, Uppsala: Šafrán and Boží Mlýn, 1982.

But this flood of texts, regardless of their quality, helped to create the cultural environment that later gave birth to great poets – such as Jáchym Topol[12] to name just one.

A typical underground poet, one comparable to Bondy and Zajíček, was Fanda Pánek. I say typical, because one of the generally perceived attributes of underground poetry was a forthrightness that made an abundant use of so-called vulgar language, or, at least, did not avoid it. In the ground-breaking years of the underground, Fanda Pánek was one of the most popular poets – indeed his poems are still enjoyed today, now that Fanda has abandoned underground circles for the twilight of some Catholic church. He may have saved his soul but I am not sure about his poetry.

Josef Vondruška was undoubtedly one of the greatest personalities of the Czech underground of the 70s. He helped establish groups Umělá hmota and Dom, which stood as the Czech equivalent to the punk movement, and by dint of his talent and determination he rose from a purely working class environment to heights that a century earlier would have earned him the description of "maudit". A friend of mine described him as "a Weiner[13] of the suburbs". Few poets here have described with such clarity the despair and hopelessness of a member of an underprivileged class, who is able to reflect on his fate and rebel against it. Although Vondruška was not included in the dictionary of Czech writers – I am obviously referring to the dictionary published by Škvorecký's *68 Publishers*[14] – he is still one of the great poets, whose significance oversteps the bounds of the

---

12) Jáchym Topol's samizdat collections of poems of the 80s have been published several times in one volume: *Miluju tě k zbláznění*, for the first time published by Atlantis, Brno, 1991. Some of Topol's early poems were translated into English. See *Yazzyk*, Issue 1, Prague, 1992, pp. 3–6 ["And then there was this spider"; "But now"]; *Yazzyk*, Issue 4, Prague, 1995, pp. 30–31 ["Game Park"].

13) Richard Weiner (1884–1937), Czech poet and novelist, Paris correspondent of the Prague newspaper *Lidové noviny* [author's note].

14) The dictionary of banned Czech writers: Jiří Brabec, Jiří Gruša, Igor Hájek, Petr Kabeš, Jan Lopatka, *Slovník českých spisovatelů. Pokus o rekonstrukci dějin české literatury 1948–1979* (Toronto: Sixty-Eight Publishers, 1982); for the second time published as *Slovník zakázaných autorů 1948–1980*, ed. Jiří Brabec et al. (Prague: SPN, 1991).

underground. He now lives in Australia, still doing manual work, and is engaged in writing the remarkable *Letters to Egon Bondy*.[15]

Other poets I mentioned in connection with the first anthology, Stankovič, Jirousová, and Brabenec are not so easily classifiable as "underground" compared to Bondy, Zajíček, Pánek, or Vondruška. Were it not for their own designation, nobody would think of classifying them as such. The first of them, Stankovič, was the only one to gain certain recognition as poet – he used to be editor of *Tvář*[16] where some of his poems were published. He belongs to the underground because of his close personal ties with its protagonists. His esoteric poetry, which is, anyway, difficult to locate inside the context of Czech literature, otherwise does not display the above-mentioned features. It is a witty, nonsense poetry, an artfulness, revelled in assonances and monstrous puns, in which Stankovič, with his fantastic gift of imagination and tireless ability to create rhymed variations, incessantly dreams up bizarre textual disfigurations – and his texts are only part of a stream of a sound he perpetually creates almost automatically.

While it was somewhat difficult to incorporate Stankovič's early poetry into the underground, this obviously does not apply to the situation in the 80s, when he earned respect among the so-called "second underground generation". In 1985 he edited a compilation from the first books of poetry by authors born in the 50s and 60s which was entitled *Už na to seru, protože to mám za pár* (I couldn't give a fuck, 'cos I'm out in a couple of days). But that anthology was published in a completely different situation. Let's go back to 1975.

The remaining poets, namely Věra Jirousová and Vratislav Brabenec, made their debut at that time with a mature poetic oeuvre that was so distinctive and individual that it did not spawn any succession. The poems of Jirousová, manneristically honed in seclusion from the world, indifferent to public response, have been rarely

---

15) Vondruška's *Letters to Egon Bondy*: So far, the selected *Letters* have only been published in a journal; see Josef Vondruška, "Dopisy Egonu Bondymu", *Paternoster* 26 (Vienna: 1989). Vondruška returned to Prague in the mid 90s where he went on writing his memoirs and made a number of remarkable collages. He died there in 2014.
16) A substantial part of articles and texts published in *Tvář* magazine (1964-1965, 1968-1969) has recently been included in one book volume: *Tvář. Výbor z* časopisu; edited by Michael Špirit (Prague: Torst, 1995).

published – with the exception of Expedice[17] – and they are unlikely ever to become the object of mass adoration. As for Brabenec – he achieved popularity as the saxophonist of the Plastic People and the author of their two lengthy compositions – *Jak bude po smrti* (How it will be after death),[18] a paraphrase of texts by Ladislav Klíma,[19] and *Co znamená vésti koně* (Leading Horses).[20] With the exception of one text by Pavel Zajíček, they are all Brabenec's poems set to music. In general, Brabenec has been regarded more as a musician, or more accurately, his poetry was appreciated and respected but he never became a "popular" poet like Bondy or Pánek.

As I am talking about the first phase of the Czech underground – more or less the situation in the 70s – I will make an attempt to describe its atmosphere. First and foremost, I have no intention to claim that the underground was the only important cultural stratum of that period. That was why Bondy and myself started to use the term "second culture" – as a counterpart to the official "first" culture. The "second culture" encompassed all unofficial output, including the underground. There were of course many other authors who had been forced into illegality at the beginning of the 70s for their political or simply moral stands. However, their work had a different character than the output of the underground and although we later became friends with many of them, we were always distinct to a certain extent.

Until the trial in 1976, the underground itself led a relatively separate existence. Its medium, the rock music of the Plastic People, DG 307 and other groups, created in the surrounding avowedly hostile world a spiritual enclave, where the bonds of friendship

17) 16 Expedice: the samizdat edition, established by Václav Havel. See its bibliography: Jiří Gruntorád, "Edice Expedice", *Kritický sborník*, XIV, no. 3 (1994), pp. 66–78; no. 4 (1994), pp. 71–80; see Jitka Hanáková, *Edice českého samizdatu*, (Prague: Národní knihovna České republiky, 1997); Gabriela Romanová, *Příběh Edice Expedice* (Prague: Knihovna Václava Havla, 2014).
18) See note 11 to Wilson's essay published in this volume.
19) Ladislav Klíma (1878-1928), Czech anti-positivist philosopher, influenced by Schopenhauer and Nietzsche [author's note].
20) Released on LP in Toronto by Boží Mlýn [author's note]. More recently released on a CD: Plastic People of the Universe, *Co znamená vésti koně* [*Leading Horses*]: PPU VII., 1981 (Prague: Globus Music, 2002).

were so deep that there cannot be any hope that these idyllic times would ever return. Bondy's book *Invalidní sourozenci* (The Disabled Siblings)[21] transposed this world into the realm of a fairy tale and, in return, it influenced the self-consciousness of the underground as an autonomous minority, which, *outside* the official world of the establishment, attempted to create a structure that can be in the full sense of the word described as parallel, although this term was first introduced into Czech culture some years later.

The orientation of the underground of the 70s was significantly influenced by a meeting with the circle connected to the banned and defunct magazine *Tvář* – Jiří Němec, Jan Lopatka, Zbyněk Hejda, Andrej Stankovič; or perhaps it was the fact that the underground approach to creativity was in tune with the artistic stances that *Tvář* had once favoured. In the literary underground – the situation in rock music was somehow different – the point was not to create artifacts (which was and is the aim of the majority of writers, who after 1969 shifted from officialdom into illegality), but rather to employ art in order to create a world of different values that could be inhabited by those who did not fit into the plans of the establishment. I tried to write something on this matter in my *Report on the Third Czech Musical Revival*, which, to a great extent, helped mould the next generation of the underground, particularly in terms of determining the non-conformist attitudes of young people.

Charter 77, which was drafted as a response to the trial of members of the Czech underground in 1976, gave rise to the emergence of a much broader community, within which personal relationships were, at least in the first years, undoubtedly as deep and spiritually rich as in the underground. Nevertheless, the underground continued to preserve its own specific characteristics, although it is difficult to define them.

What characterised it above all was that it defied classification or manipulation and that it consciously or subconsciously tended to occupy a position on the margins of society. I cannot resist illustrating the essential attitude of the underground by the ingenious answer of Olga Havlová in a book of interviews with twelve Czech

---

21) Bondy's novel *Invalidní sourozenci*: see note 19 to Jirous's text *Report on the third Czech Musical Revival*, published in this volume.

women by Eva Kantůrková.[22] There Eva asks Olga something like: "I have heard they are people who would not succeed in any society, even abroad." And Olga answers: "And why should they succeed? Is life supposed to be some kind of competition?"

Persecution of the underground did not end with the trial in 1976. Police pressure on the underground never ceased to exist because virtually everyone who professed to be a member of the underground had signed Charter 77. During the period of the worst repression, i.e. 1980–1981, Sváťa Karásek, Vráťa Brabenec, Josef Vondruška, Pavel Zajíček, Jaroslav Bowie Unger, Tomáš Liška, Zina Freundová, Aleš Březina, Miroslav Skalický, Karel Havelka, Jiří Němec and many other activists of the Czech underground emigrated.

It seemed for a while that the Czech underground would never recover from this blow, especially when at the end of 1981 the establishment again imprisoned František Stárek-Čuňas, myself, and Milan Hýbek; the publisher Jiří Gruntorád was already in jail and a number of underground activists would sooner or later also end up in prison.

But in 1985 – in the middle of the most marasmic decade of "Real Socialism" in Czechoslovakia – the first issue of samizdat *Revolver Revue* was published. Within its pages the so-called "second underground generation" – Ivan Lamper, Jáchym Topol, Petr Placák,[23] Anna Wágnerová, J. H. Krchovský,[24] and many other poets and novelists

22) Interview with Olga Havlová: see Eva Kantůrková, *Sešly jsme se v této knize*, first published in Czech by Index, Köln 1980, then in 1991 by Toužimský a Moravec, Praha (interview with O. H.: pp. 5–15); the book was also published in French *Douze femmes à Prague* (Paris: Maspero, 1981), and in German, *Verbotene Bürger. Die Frauen der Charta 77* (Munich: Langen-Müller, 1982).

23) A selection of Petr Placák's samizdat poetry of the 80s has been published in one volume: *Obrovský zasněžený hřbitov* (Prague: Torst, 1995). His novel *Medorek* has been published five times in different samizdat editions between 1985–1989, then three times in the form of a printed book: *Medorek* (Prague: Lidové noviny– Česká expedice, 1990); *Medorek* (Prague: Hynek, 1997); *Medorek* (Prague: Plus, 2010).

24) J. H. Krchovský's samizdat collections of poems of the 80s have been published several times, first in three volumes: *Noci, po nichž nepřichází ráno* (Brno: Host, 1991); *Leda s labutí* (Brno: Host, 1997); *Dodatky* (Brno: Host, 1997); more recently in: *Básně* (Brno: Host, 1998); *Básně sebrané* (Brno: Host, 2010). Some of Krchovský's poems were translated into English. See his *Seven poems* (Trans. by Justin Quinn), in *METRE* [Magazine of international poetry], Hull–Praha–Dublin, Autumn 2001. Some more

started to speak out with unsuspected incisiveness. The significant sociological shift I mentioned at the beginning of these comments took place inside this generation. These were no longer simply up-rooted workers or rockers, but young intellectuals with a distinct orientation, who started to occupy a new and completely distinctive role not within Czech culture, but on the European scene as a whole. Jáchym Topol, who is also present at this New York conference, has described the situation so accurately and in such detail in his paper, that I would only repeat his words.

Written in Prague in March 1990.
[Translated by Tomáš Liška]

poems by Krchovský in English translation (by Marek Tomin and Howard Sidenberg) appear in a booklet added to the record by the Plastic People of the Universe: *Líně s tebou spím / Lazy Love. In Memoriam Milan Hlavsa*, (Prague: Globus Music, 2001). [Bylo to nedávno / Recently, Teď už vím / Now I know, Sen o hadech / Snake Dream, Spáč / The Sleeper, Moc jsem si neužil / It wasn't such a Blast.] The text Šílenství (Madness) appears in Czech and in English in the booklet added to the record Milan Hlavsa: *Šílenství / Madness* (Prague: Globus Music, 1999).

Jáchym Topol
The Story of Revolver Revue

CONTRIBUTION TO A CLOSER UNDERSTANDING
OF THE LAST SAMIZDAT GENERATION

Since 1985 I have been involved in the publication of *Revolver Revue*, which is why I intend to concentrate on independent literary publication in Czechoslovakia, with special references to that part of it which is virtually unknown abroad, and about which even the intellectuals in Czechoslovakia – i.e. those who, with the exception of the police were the only ones to pay serious attention to samizdat – were not particularly aware of.

In the textbooks that will be written one day, whole generations will coalesce into a solid mass from which only individuals will emerge. Similarly, when viewed from abroad, literary activities in Czechoslovakia must have looked like a strange and exotic battle of the banned and the permitted, while the background of dissident literature remained obscured. In fact, in the vaults, in the world of the banned, all kinds of space existed: cellars, corners and secret corridors, in which various groups, coteries and individuals lived and held sway.

That part of dissent I am concerned with – the part described for simplicity's sake as "the underground", or even "the second generation of the underground" – had to capture its publishing space at the beginning of the eighties. The group I belong to as an author and publisher entered an inhabited territory in which a whole number of different illegal editions were already operating. Specialised literary journals were already being published; history, philosophy and journalism were flourishing independent of the policies of the regime's publishing houses.[1]

Despite this, or precisely because of it, I want to look at it from the point of view of my generation, whether there was any difference between us – i.e. those who weren't driven or thrown into the world of the banned, but were simply born into it – and those

---

1) About the samizdat periodicals, see Johanna Posset, *Tschechische Samizdat-Periodika 1968–1988*, (Vienna: Universität Wien, Diplomarbeit, 1990); Johanna Posset, *Česká samizdatová periodika 1968–1989* (Brno: Reprografia, 1991); Vilém Prečan, *Bibliography of the Czechoslovak Samizdat: Samizdat periodicals 1977–1988*, in: ACTA, vol. 2, no. 5–8, Winter 1988 (Scheinfeld: Dokumentationzentrum); Blahoslav Dokoupil, *Slovník českých literárních časopisů, periodických literárních sborníků a almanachů 1945–2000* (Brno-Olomouc: Host-Votobia, 2002).

who belonged to that already existing sphere that some of us tentatively described as "the established underground" or even the "underground establishment". After all, we are the last generation of samizdat and the first generation for which one of the main themes in the works of our predecessors and older contemporaries – the brutal interruption of the entire country's development in 1968 – was already no more than an echo.

For the sake of simplicity and in order to make my investigation easier I shall often be using the plural. In doing so, I fully realize the snags involved. I am completely aware of the inadequacy of such expressions as "my generation" or "the group I belong to". Indeed whenever I use them, I have in my memory the faces of actual people, their shared characteristics. Nonetheless, I shall be dealing with certain special features of the times that none of us eluded, and which therefore could apply to everyone, as well as the atmosphere of those days with its bans and limitations that affected absolutely everyone who did any writing. I shall also devote some attention to those who overstepped those limitations. And the creation of the journal *Revolver Revue* and the group of Czech writers it attracted appear to be a good starting point for my investigation.

There is one thing we were always aware of: the fact that we were in the opposition. And if it ever slipped from people's memory, it took no more than a police interrogation to bring it back to them. What went without saying was a deep dissatisfaction with the regime and a reluctance to publish in its publishing houses. Even more significant in my view, and what directly led to the creation of *Revolver Revue* and its book series was a natural dissatisfaction with the situation in samizdat. It seemed to us that despite the enormous number of excellent books published in the established samizdat editions like Vaculík's *Petlice*[2] (Padlock Books) or Havel's *Expedice*, the active radius of those operations was extremely limited. These were writers' enterprises conceived for writers. And even though we admired them, we wanted to work in a different way. Furthermore our situation was quite different – and in that respect the Polish model was quite influential. The point is that the Poles

---

2) *Edice Petlice* was founded by Ludvík Vaculík in 1972; see its bibliography in *ACTA*, 1987/3-4, Scheinfeld; also in: *Nové knihy*, 1990, no. 7-23.

were able to bring out books in print runs of several thousands, not just Solidarity's political pamphlets, but also literature. Those of us who had passports – or so long as we had them – used to travel to Poland to study the way they operated. In more recent years we would go to Hungary. On the way there and back we used to smuggle literature in the form of books by banned authors. People would cross the frontiers illicitly, taking mountain trails, in order to fetch books and journals, and more recently to bring back instructional videocassettes. I will never forget the time when a Polish border guard caught us, the amazement on his face when he looked inside my rucksack and found it full of books: "You're mad. You've got no vodka or salami. You're crazy!"

And we were crazy. We managed to print sixty copies of the first issue of *Revolver Revue*. It seemed an enormous number at the time – good for a start. From the outset we wanted to publish a journal for the general public, not just for the benefit of a small circle of readers or the exile publishers. For that reason the model we chose was different from that of the older underground journal: *Vokno*, edited by František Stárek.[3] Unfortunately he was then in prison and *Vokno*'s future was uncertain – we also realised that our styles were different. We criticised other publishers for the tiny size of their print runs, sometimes only one set of typed copies. The 12 or 16 copies that could be produced that way meant that such editions were far too exclusive. We realised that although we had grown up in the same traditions as those who were twenty or thirty years our senior, spiritually we were somewhere else.

Above all we were the first generation of authors since 1948 not to have known any sort of life but what the Communists called Socialism. We were stokers, window-cleaners, night watchmen and drawers of disability pensions just like our fathers and grandfathers and we resembled them in biological and spiritual terms, but with one important exception: we had never known anything else. And for years we never believed we would know anything else. We were stuck forever in the underworld we had entered as teenagers. None

---

3) About *Vokno*, see bibliographies mentioned in note 1; more detailed information see in: Jana Růžková – Jiří Gruntorád, "Samizdatový časopis *Vokno*", in: *Kritický sborník*, XIX, 1999/2000, pp. 193–231.

of us knew anything of literary glory and the thought of our books on a bookshop counter was absurd and laughable. None of us shared the experience of those authors who formed the backbone of banned literature: men and women who were honoured by the nation, whose faces and books had been familiar in the sixties. The younger and youngest writers were surrounded by enormous silence. Apart from official hacks, no literary critics paid them the slightest regard.

Now a bit of pre-history.

I don't remember much about 1968. I just have a vague memory of tanks and guns in the Prague streets, but my principal recollection of that turning point dates from slightly later. I can remember very well how we used to address our primary school teachers as "Mr" or "Mrs". That all changed overnight. Teachers were now to be addressed uniformly as "Comrade". We stubbornly stuck to the old form of address and those teachers who did not reprimand or punish us for it soon disappeared from school. I had first hand experience of the process of rewriting history. 1968 was year zero. We were all schizophrenics. We heard one thing at home and something totally different at school. We were all nasty little Švejks who learnt how to live very well within that duality. And later we were to end up sitting beneath all sorts of Švejks made from wood or wire – in the pub. There can hardly be a better-liked or hated literary figure in Bohemia and a representation of him hangs in every bar.

During the years I have been editing poetry for *Revolver Revue*, many verse collections have passed through my hands, but I have never heard of a single literary group being founded, in the sense of the associations, literary circles, clubs or other groupings that were a living tradition in the Czech lands from at least the nineteen-twenties. If you were to emerge from the underground and form a group of that kind, it would have been regarded by your warders as an attempt to create an illegal cell threatening Socialism. And the system of bureaucratic and administrative bans totally ruled out any free public activity. A recital of juvenile poetry risked to be cut short due to an invasion of marauding goons. And, indeed, it used to happen from time to time. There was nowhere for us to hold regular meetings and it never occurred to us to establish some group with its own programme and rules. We met one another mostly in pubs or apartments. Or at concerts. We knew the names of banned authors and sometimes managed to get to see them. Maybe what appealed to us the most at first was not so much their literary achievement but their strength of character and their capacity to resist. It was only about a twenty-minute walk from where I lived at the time to the flat of Egon Bondy, the author of dozens of books that circulated in typewritten copies. I had read them and copied them out myself and believed him to be dead – so total was our isolation. That twenty-minute walk to Egon Bondy's took me four years.

But ours was not a dead-end situation. Those who entered the vault of banned literature at an early age, unencumbered by family ties and without the burden of former literary glory had plenty of opportunities to work, familiarize themselves with new technologies and try to beat new paths, and there were plenty in that category. In 1976, the police arrested the most underground of rock bands: The Plastic People of the Universe, along with a lot of their fans. The regime's aim was to destroy those underground spaces of free creation. It was then that other banned and silenced people from other spheres, from other passages of the ghetto, closed ranks in their defence. Charter 77 came into being and a wave of persecution followed. I was fifteen at the time.

There was no entry ticket into the underground. Entry was natural and gradual. After their release, the Plastics went on organizing concerts; I managed to get into one of them and immediately found myself in a world of adventure. It was as if the humiliating schizophrenia of school life just ceased to exist. Boredom and the grey of the streets – broken only by the red of the banners – no longer dominated my life. I discovered the existence of another world in which it was possible to work, in which work had a point – and it was a world of adventure to boot. I did not give a thought to human rights. I did not give a thought to socialism, or capitalism, or revolution, or the market economy; not even to free speech – they were nothing but ludicrous abstract notions as far as I was concerned. It did offer some space to work in. Here was a world of conspiratorial messages, bugged telephones, secret rendezvous, secret rock concerts, secret seminars on literature and philosophy where banned teachers and banned students came together. It was a world where one diced with danger – but it was not boring. It was not the boring and unpleasant intermezzo of school that was bound to give way to normality. It was a reality that had no comparison for us anywhere because we had had no experience of normality.

My aim here is to describe the atmosphere, the undergrowth, from which literary works were later to spring. It was there that I first met the subsequent authors, editors, typists and peddlers of *Revolver Revue*. We came to know the literature of the fifties: the diaries of Jan Hanč,[4] the poetry of Jiří Kolář[5] – an author who had been jailed in the fifties for a book that was due to be printed for the first time in 1968 or 69, but ended up being pulped, of course; it was not until the eighties that we printed an excerpt from it, as a group of young enthusiasts, and we were aware of that continuity. We soon discovered that even the normal freedom of the sixties was not without snags: *Revolver Revue* was the first to publish the poetry of Jana Krejcarová,[6] a poetess from the Midnight group – also of the fifties – whose verse even caused consternation among dissident readers in 1984 on account of its alleged pornographic nature. (Incidentally, she is best known here under the name of Jana Černá as the author of reminiscences about her mother Milena Jesenská).[7] We read the dictionary of banned Czech authors put out by Josef Škvorecký.[8] We did not care that some of the works to which it referred were unavailable. The very fact of reading the authors' autobiographies was an adventure.

The fate of books that were successively banned, permitted and then banned again matched the fate of their authors. It made fantastic reading! Nothing could have contrasted more starkly with the uniform greyness of officially permitted journals.

I already mentioned the work of Jan Hanč. It is as if Czech literature lived on in writers' diaries. You can see it in the mature writing

---

4) Jan Hanč's complete works were published for the first time in one volume: Jan Hanč, *Události* (Prague: Československý spisovatel, 1991).

5) Jiří Kolář's collected works were published in nine volumes: *Dílo Jiřího Koláře 1-9* (Praha-Litomyšl: Odeon-Mladá fronta-Paseka, 1992-2000).

6) About the editions of Krejcarová's poetical works see note 5 to Bondy's essay published in this volume.

7) See Jana Černá, *Kafka's Milena*, trans. A. G. Brain (London: Souvenir Press, 1988).

8) See note 14 to Jirous's New York lecture published in this volume.

of Zbyněk Hejda[9] or Ludvík Vaculík's brilliant *Czech Dreambook*.[10] Traces of it are evident in the autobiographical undertones of some of Havel's plays. And those are all experienced writers. For me and other contributors to *Revolver Revue*, the most important task of all was to capture events, to describe life as we knew it – quite simply to get it down on paper. Producing literature was not the immediate task.

Everything I have tried to describe here in only a few pages was described almost faultlessly by Petr Placák in the 200 pages or thereabouts of his novel *Medorek*.[11] Even the process of producing a magazine – all the effort and risk involved, including the atmosphere of a free creative process in totalitarian encirclement – seemed more important than the successive issues of the magazine itself. In this connection one can observe the greatest danger of this type of work: self-absorption, lack of competition, isolation.

We wanted to escape – into the world. There was no way to cross the wire – well, maybe there was, but it would have meant staying on the other side forever. But we wanted to stay and work. One of the slogans of *Revolver Revue* was "off ghetto magazine".[12] We started to concentrate on translations. In a country where Henry Miller was last published in 1968 and Louis Ferdinand Céline in 1947, literary

9) Zbyněk Hejda's complete poetical works were first published in five volumes (*Sbírky Zbyňka Hejdy 1–5*, Prague: KDM, 1992–1993), and later in one volume: Zbyněk Hejda: *Básně*, (Prague: Torst, 1996).

10) Ludvík Vaculík's "diary-novel" Český *snář* was published for the first time by Sixty-Eight Publishers (Toronto, 1983); in the author's native country it was published several times in samizdat and then, in 1990, by Atlantis, Brno. The novel has been translated by Gerald Turner and awaits publication. Excerpts from the translation were published in the international literary review *Trafika* 3, Summer 1994. Previously excerpts from *A Czech Dream Book*, translated and introduced by Michael Henry Heim, were published in *Cross Currents* (Ann Arbor: University of Michigan, 1984) 71–86. An interpretation of Vaculík's book can be found in Helena Sedláčková-Gibbs' work: *Moral Politics and Its Others: The Charter 77 Dissident Movement in Czechoslovakia (1977–1989)*. (A dissertation submitted to the Department of Comparative Literature, New York University, May 2003).

11) About Placák's novel *Medorek*, see note 23 to Jirous's New York lecture published in this volume.

12) An actual English subtitle of one of the samizdat issues of Revolver Revue; it meant to say, "a magazine outside the [political, social] ghetto".

translation represented an enormous territory, an untapped wealth that we pounced on with enthusiasm.

And gradually the ice started to melt. Which is not to say that one could not go to jail for samizdat activity. In the first issue of *Revolver Revue*, as a tribute to Ivan Jirous, we published his verse collection *Magor's Swan Songs*,[13] which had been smuggled out of prison by Jiří Gruntorád (who was, by coincidence, also jailed for samizdat activity), and when we were producing the last underground issue of the magazine, Jirous was inside yet again. Admittedly they could jail us whenever they liked, but by 1988 things were no longer what they were in 1978. Among other things, that fact helped us to become familiar with more efficient reproduction techniques and thumb our noses at our fathers' typewriters. The regime had its hands full with the political opposition and left such spectres as Allen Ginsberg, Victorian pornography, Hannah Arendt's essays, Timothy Garton Ash's articles, the prose and poetry of banned Czech and Slovak authors, and neglected and unpublished foreign authors alone for the time being, as something they would find time to sort out later.

And the regime's confusion could be felt. Changes were in the air and we started to entertain hopes that the era of banned literature truly was no more than an intermezzo. Various writers from official circles started showing an interest – some of them in order to furnish themselves in time with an alibi, some of them also had enough of the divided literature game. We even started receiving the first offers of publication for young authors. But such offers were turned down by all those in the *Revolver Revue* circle.

We had thirteen issues behind us.[14] Our biggest issue was 450 pages long. We were even publishing books. In association with

13) Ivan Martin Jirous's collection of prison poems *Magorovy labutí písně* was published several times in samizdat between 1985–1989; first printed in 1986 by the Czech exile publishing house PmD, in Munich, Germany. Since 1989 it has been published several times, e.g. in I. M. Jirous, *Magorova summa* (Prague: Torst, 1998, 2007, 2015).

14) About *Revolver Revue*, see bibliographies mentioned in note 1; more detailed information see in: Vlastimil Ježek, *Bibliografie Revolver Revue 1–13*, in: *Kritický sborník*, XI, 1991, no. 3, no. 4. See also: http://scriptum.cz/cs/periodika/revolver-revue -jednou-nohou.

the already associated editorial group of the political journal *Sport*, we started to publish *Information Service*[15] as the only regularly appearing opposition newspaper. We are still continuing to publish *Revolver Revue*. The magazine's pages are open to all authors, though naturally we intend to go on publishing authors who helped shape the magazine so far. I have already mentioned Petr Placák; we are bringing out his book under the symbolic title of *Trips in Search of Adventure*.[16] Then there is Miroslav Ptáček who had managed to write a whole number of things before committing suicide; we are planning to bring them out in a collected edition under the title of *Adieu and a Chain*;[17] Anna Wágnerová, who came to readers' attention with her feminist poetry, published some years ago under the justifiably immodest title of *Performance of Genius*;[18] Václav Bauman, whose novel *Pat-A-Cake, Pat-A-Cake Baker's Man*, caused quite a commotion when it was published some time ago in *Revolver Revue*,[19] for having dared with brutal frankness to describe the life of Prague homosexuals and thereby break a taboo that applied in official and unofficial literature alike. It could even be that Ještěrka (Lizard),[20]

15) A bibliography of *Informační servis* magazine was published on a CD: *Respekt '90–00: deset let*, (Prague: Respekt, 2000).

16) Petr Placák's short stories *Cestou za dobrodružstvím* [Trips in Search of Adventure] were published in selection under the title *Královský hrad*, *Revolver Revue*, 14, 1990; subsequently, reworked and extended, as *Cestou za dobrodružstvím* (Prague: Babylon, 2000).

17) Only a few of Miroslav Ptáček's poems have been published since 1989; see *Na střepech volnosti. Almanach umlčené české poezie*, ed. Jaromír Hořec, (Prague: Československý spisovatel, 1991).

18) A few of Anna Wágnerová [Beatrice Landovská]'s poems have been published since 1989; see *Na střepech volnosti. Almanach umlčené české poezie*, ed. Jaromír Hořec, (Prague: Československý spisovatel, 1991). Her collection of poems *Geniální vystoupení* [*Performance of Genius*] was published only 23 years later (Prague: Aula, 2013).

19) Václav Bauman [František Růžička]'s novel *Paci, paci, pacičky* [*Pat-A-Cake, Pat-A-Cake Baker's Man*] was published in samizdat and then twice by regular printing presses: Prague: Scéna, 1990; Prague: Akropolis, 2017.

20) Ještěrka's text *Narkomanka* was published only in samizdat (*Revolver Revue*, 13, 1989). The text was sent anonymously to the editors of *Revolver Revue* in 1989. Its author, an unknown drug-addict, probably from the North Bohemian town of Teplice, published no further texts, at least not under the pseudonym of Ještěrka.

the pseudonym of a woman writer who described in the form of an addict's diary the underworld jungle of industrial North Bohemia, will finally surface. We are publishing *Ship's Log*, a prose work by the macabre humorist Vít Kremlička[21] who has previously published stories and verse in samizdat. We are planning a new edition of the works of J. H. Krchovský,[22] a decadent writer whose work draws on the early twentieth century school of Czech writing, and whose titles include the epic *Travelling Mummy* and various collections with a gloomy feel to them, the most recent being *Waltz with My Shadow*: he has no intention of abandoning his pseudonym of "Undertaker",[23] even after the revolution. We are currently preparing a selection of Kamil K. Kuchyňka's caustically ironic short stories.[24] Another author of short stories is J. Teufel,[25] whose range is truly extensive from descriptions of a stoker's work to the demolishing of national myths such as in the text entitled *Interview with Dubček*. And there are a

---

21) Vít Kremlička's experimental prose *Lodní deník* [*Ship's Log*] was published in samizdat and then by regular printing presses: Prague: NTS, 1991; five poems from Kremlička's post 1990 collection of poems *Cizrna* (Prague: Torst, 1995) were published in English translation in the Prague based English magazine *OPTIMISM*, 35, 1999 [translation by Petra Vachunová, editors Laura Conway and Tim Otis]. Three other poems in English translation appeared in the San Francisco based international literary magazine *WATCHWORD* (issue 2, Winter 2001) [translation by Pavla Niklová and Laura Conway].

22) J. H. Krchovský's poetry collections have not been published by RR since 1989; see note 24 to Jirous's New York lecture published in this volume.

23) The pseudonym Krchovský is a tricky one: besides other allusions it hides in itself the slang Czech-German word "krchov" which is "Kirchhof" in German, and means "churchyard" or "cemetery" in English. Hence the poet's pseudonym could also be translated as "Graveyard".

24) Kamil K. Kuchyňka [Vladimír Jurásek]'s short stories were published only in samizdat (e.g. *Džez, První pomoc, Námluvy*, in: Revolver Revue / Jednou nohou, 6, 1987). Jurásek is actually a rock musician who played with underground rock bands, e.g. Classic Rock'n'Roll Band, and Garáž, see e.g. the record *The Best of Garáž* (Prague: Globus International, 1990). His only further publication after 1990 was a short story *Příběh pytlíkový*, in: Playboy [Czech edition], 8, 1992, which appeared under the author's own name.

25) The mentioned texts by Josef Teufel [*Ivo Železný* – not to be mistaken with the renowned Czech publisher of the same name!] were probably published only in samizdat.

whole lot of other writers whose works have been so far published only in minimal print runs in persecuted journals – authors about whom I have tried to tell you something, and who are generally referred to as the "second underground generation". It only remains to add that they could equally justify the title of: "writers of the last underground generation".

Prague – New York 1990
[Translated by Gerald Turner 1990]

The content of the volume *Views from the Inside: Czech Underground Literature and Culture (1948-1989)* speaks clearly by itself and for itself, so it hardly needs to be commented on extensively. Recently there has been growing interest in the given subject on the part of foreign students coming to the Czech Republic to study its history, culture, and literature, though lacking knowledge of the Czech language. Although there has been relatively a lot written and published in English on the theme of Czech dissidence, the Charter 77 movement, Havel's "moral politics", and even on samizdat book and periodical production, including works by Skilling, Prečan, Day, Tucker, Gibbs, Falk and Bolton (see bibliography), relatively little information is still available on the narrower topic of the Czech (Czechoslovak) underground culture: literature, music, arts and the underground movement as such, with its historical, sociological, psychological background. Most of the authors (both Czech and English or American ones) have so far paid little attention to the rich variety of Czech underground culture (and if so, then mainly with regards to its political role: such as the fact that the trial of the members of the Plastic People in 1976 provided the impetus for Charter 77), perhaps also because of this variety, the intricate structure of Czech underground culture has been neglected. Is it up to the historians of (rock) music, or up to the sociologists, or up to the historians of Czech literature, or up to art historians – to deal with this subject? Some of these doubts may be removed by this volume, but there certainly remains one obstacle preventing the English-reading public from perceiving what the Czech underground really was about, at least as far as its literary production is concerned. Although dozens and maybe even hundreds of editions and publications of Czech underground literature have been published in the original Czech since 1989, thus enabling at least several of the best known underground writers to be incorporated into the main body of Czech literature (Bondy, Vodseďálek, Krejcarová, Knížák, Stankovič, Jirous, Zajíček, Karásek, Krchovský, Jáchym Topol, Petr Placák), so far there has been little opportunity for these writers to enter the Anglo-American literary scene: with the notable exception of Jáchym Topol's post-1990 prose writings, especially his novel *City Sister Silver* (Catbird Press, North Haven, CT, 2000; transl. by Alex

Zucker). However, yet another exception, the volume containing all the poems put into music by the Plastic People – in good English translation (see bibliography), has been largely ignored both by translators and Anglo-American publishers, or by the abovementioned historians of political dissidence.

As for the music of the best known Czech underground rock groups and experimental ensembles, such as the Plastic People of the Universe, Aktual, DG 307, etc., the situation seems to be far better now, especially thanks to the editor Jaroslav Riedel who spent years carefully editing and remastering the primitive, rough recordings of the music, which were subsequently issued on a series of CD's (see discography).

Now, with this volume, English-speaking readers have an opportunity to learn something about the Czech underground movement as such, about its political and ideological background, about its ambitions and main ideas, and also about some of its literary works. Here it is the leading figures of the Czech underground themselves who address the English-speaking reader. These are no literary or art historians standing outside the underground cultural and literary scene (although Ivan Jirous was educated as an art historian, and Egon Bondy spent the 80s writing a voluminous history of philosophy): instead they are witnesses giving evidence, providing testimonies – subjective and possibly biased, but extraordinarily valuable for the same reason.

However, there was at least one more reason why we thought the present volume should comprise the five texts included. Although all of the texts were translated into (or written in) English some time ago, only two of them were published and none of them has been available to English-speaking readers for a long time, if ever. The five texts also represent at least three different approaches to the given subject, thus unconsciously demonstrating the variety of the underground literary scene.

Jirous's *Report*, probably the most important text out of the five included, was written in 1975 and its author conceived it as a sort of apologia, or manifesto – an articulation of the underground movement's aims, and a description of its – then – short history. It was undoubtedly written mainly for Czech readers, first of all for the members of the underground community, as a sort of a feedback, but also for all samizdat readers – to give them a chance to learn what the "dreaded underground" was really about, and last but not least – let us not forget it! – its author also had to take "unwelcome readers" into account: the Czechoslovak authorities, the *kulturträgers*, the police censors and the interrogators of the totalitarian era (in this respect the text should be read and interpreted in the same way as all the subsequent Charter 77 declarations). In its English translation it was published in a booklet/catalogue *The Merry Ghetto*, included with the first record of the Plastic People of the Universe *Egon Bondy's Happy Hearts Club Banned*, Paris – London, 1978; it was translated from the Czech original, entitled *Zpráva o třetím českém hudebním obrození*, by Paul Wilson and Ivan Hartel. In Czech it was published several times in samizdat editions, more recently in an edition of Jirous's collected essays, critiques, and reviews *Magorův zápisník*, ed. Michael Špirit, Torst, Praha, 1997 and in *"Hnědá kniha" o procesech s českým undergroundem*, ed. Martin Machovec, ÚSTR, Praha 2012. Excerpts from the *Report* (translated by Eric Dluhosch) were published in the volume *Primary Documents. A Sourcebook for Eastern and Central European Art since the 1950s*; ed. Laura Hoptman and Tomáš Pospiszyl, The Museum of Modern Art, New York, NY, 2002. Jirous' *Report* was also published in French, German, Polish, and Russian translations.

Wilson's text *What's it like…*, written in English in 1983, has a very different purpose from Jirous's *Report*: it is a bit nostalgic, looking back at the never-to-return times; it is the author's memoirs, and it was certainly written for Canadian, American, and British readers, especially those interested in the international rock scene. The article was apparently published in the magazine *Musician*, February 1983, but the editor had at his disposal only a photocopy of the pages with its text, and no title page of the periodical, so there still remain some doubts about the date of the issue. The article was soon translated into Czech, but surprisingly enough, it was published only once, in a samizdat magazine: "Jaký je to dělat rock v policejním státě? Stejný jako všude jinde, jenom těžší. O moc těžší", *Revolver Revue* , 3/4, Praha, 1986. The translator is not mentioned. Later it was published as a part of the volume *Pohledy zevnitř* (see the final paragraph of this epilogue), and in an anthology of Wilson's essays and studies translated into Czech: *Bohemian Rhapsodies*, Torst, Praha 2011.

The history of the three remaining texts seems to be more simple: In the early months of 1990 all of them were written in Czech by their authors for the purposes of a very extraordinary meeting: "Conference on Czech Literature & Culture: From Fin de Siècle to Fin de Siècle", held at New York University, March 1990. The conference, coordinated by Hana Arie Gaifman (NYU) and Peter Steiner (University of Pennsylvania) gave the first chance, after at least twenty years, to about forty former dissident and underground writers of Czechoslovakia to meet and freely discuss the issues of Czech literature. Bondy, Jirous, and Jáchym Topol read their Czech papers in an auditorium of NYU while the English translations of their papers were distributed among the English-speaking participants. The topic of their lectures was fixed in advance: Czech Underground Literature. Though they are not literary historians, it is all the more interesting to compare the results of their individual research, or rather selective evaluations, and their effort to establish some hierarchy. When reading the three texts we should not forget that in 1990 none of their authors had ever published any of their poetry or fiction, apart from samizdat books and periodicals – which differentiated them sharply from once renowned writers, quite popular in Czechoslovakia with the general reading public, such as Josef Škvorecký, Miroslav Holub, Milan Uhde, or Arnošt Lustig, all of whom were also present at the conference.

As far as we know, none of the New York conference texts in question has ever been published in English, and only two of them were published in Czech: Egon Bondy's contribution in its Czech original, under the title *Kořeny českého literárního undergroundu v letech 1949-1953*, was published altogether three times: in the magazine *Vokno*, 18, Praha, 1990; the magazine *Haňťa Press*, 8, Praha, 1990; and in a propaedeutic anthology of Czech texts *Antologie textů ke studiu* české *literatury po roce 1945*, eds. Iva Málková, Martin Pilař, Ostravská univerzita, Ostrava, 1996. Ivan Jirous's contribution in its Czech original, under the title *O české undergroundové literatuře 70. a 80. let*, was published twice: in the magazine *Vokno*, 18, Praha, 1990, and in the magazine *Iniciály*, 8-9, Praha, 1990. Jáchym Topol's contribution had very probably never been published before 2006 – either in Czech or in English. Its Czech original was never available to the editor.

This new edition of the volume *Views from the Inside* is actually already the third edition, as after the 2006 English version there followed its Czech version in 2008. The book *Pohledy zevnitř* (Pistorius & Olšanská, Praha, 2008) comprises all five texts from *Views*: Jirous' and Bondy's are found there in their Czech originals, Wilson's essay in its old samizdat translation mentioned above, and Topol's essay, the Czech original of which is lost, had to be translated back to Czech from its English translation published in *Views*, 2006, and authorized.

For this new English edition of *Views* all the texts were revised and a number of footnotes were corrected, extended and also added; information in them having been brought up-to-date. So were the sections of Bibliography, Discography and the list of documentary films.

Underground literature and culture
Czech dissidence with regards to Czech underground culture
Samizdat book/periodical production

AKTUAL: děti bolševizmu / Kids of Bolshevism, a CD, Louny: Guerilla Records, 2005. [The booklet accompanying the CD contains some of Milan Knížák's lyrics written for the band Aktual, both in Czech original and in English translation.]

Beale, Lewis: *The Rockers Who Started a Revolution*, in Herald Tribune, 16 January 2002.

Bohumil Hrabal (1914–1997). Papers from a Symposium. Edited by David Short, London: SEES, University College, 2004.

Bolton, Jonathan: *Worlds of Dissent. Charter 77, The Plastic People of the Universe, and Czech Culture under Communism*, Cambridge and London: Harvard University Press, 2012.

Bondy, Egon: *Cellar Work [Sklepní práce*, an excerpt from a novella], in: *Yazzyk Magazine* 1, Prague, 1992.

Bondy, Egon: *Berta. Part Three. Section XXII [Běta*, an excerpt from a novella], in: *Yazzyk Magazine* 4, Prague, 1995.

Bondy, Egon: *The Consolation of Ontology. On the Substantial and Nonsubstantial Models* [a philosophical treatise], translated by Benjamin B. Page; Lanham–Boulder–New York–Oxford: Lexington Books, 2001. [On Egon Bondy: "Translator's Introduction (2000)".]

Brikcius, Zuzana (ed.): *Charta Story - Příběh Charty 77 / The Story of Charter 77*, Prague: Národní galerie, 2017.

Day, Barbara: *The Velvet Philosophers*, London: The Claridge Press, 1999.

Falk, Barbara J.: *The Dilemmas of Dissidence in East-Central Europe: Citizen Intellectuals and Philosopher Kings*, New York – Budapest: Central European University Press, 2003. [See Chapter 3 – "Czechoslovakia: From Interrupted to Velvet Revolution", Part "The Underground Music Scene and the Trial of the PPU".]

Goetz-Stankiewicz, Marketa (ed.): *Good-bye, Samizdat. Twenty Years of Czechoslovak Underground Writing.* With a Foreword by Timothy Garton Ash, with an Introduction "Samizdat Literature: An Introduction" by Igor Hájek [Authors: Igor Hájek, Alexander Kliment, Ivan Klíma, Pavel Kohout, Jan Trefulka, Jiří Gruša, Dominik Tatarka, Karel Pecka, Lenka Procházková, Eda Kriseová, Egon Bondy, Milan Uhde, Ludvík Vaculík, Bohumil Hrabal, Paul Wilson, Jan Patočka, Milan Jungmann, Miroslav

Kusý, Zdeněk Urbánek, Jan Lopatka, Eva Kantůrková, Jiřina Šiklová, Petr Fidelius, Václav Havel, Erazim Kohák, Ivan M. Havel (Sakateka), Zdeněk Neubauer (Sidonius), Milan Šimečka, Ladislav Hejdánek, Martin Palouš, Radim Palouš, Tomáš Halík, Zdeněk Kratochvíl], Evanston: Northwestern University Press, 1992.

Havel, Václav: *Disturbing the Peace. A Conversation with Karel Hvížďala*, transl. by Paul Wilson; New York, Knopf, Vintage Books, 1990 [the Czech original bears the title *Dálkový výslech*].

Havel, Václav: *Open Letters: Selected Writings, 1965–1990*, ed. Paul Wilson, New York, Vintage Books, 1990. [See e.g. the text "The Trial".]

Havel, Václav et al. (Keane, John, ed.): *The Power of the Powerless: Citizens against the State in Central-Eastern Europe*, Armonk: M. E. Sharpe, 1990. [See e.g. the text "Charter 77 Declaration".]

Karásek, Svatopluk: *Say No to the Devil*, Uppsala: Šafrán 78 and Boží Mlýn, 1979. [The booklet accompanying the record contains Karásek's texts in Czech original and in English translation.]

Karlík, Viktor: *Podzemní práce (Zpětný deník) / Underground Work (Retroactive Diary)*, Prague: Revolver Revue, 2012.

Klíma, Ivan: *The Unexpected Merits of Opression.* Unpublished paper read by its author at the New York conference on Czech literature and culture, New York University, March 1990. Found in the archives of Libri Prohibiti library, Prague, and in the editor's personal archives.

Knížák, Milan: *Unvollständige Dokumentation / Some Documentary. 1961–1979* [among contributions also a text by Jindřich Chalupecký in German and English translation: "Die Geschichte von Milan Knížák / The Story of Milan Knížák"], Berlin [West]: Edition Ars Viva!, 1980.

Krchovský, J. H.: *Seven poems* (Translated from the Czech by Justin Quinn), in: METRE [Magazine of international poetry]; Hull–Praha–Dublin, Autumn 2001.

Krchovský, J. H.: Chosen poems translated by Marek Tomin; in a booklet added to the record of the Plastic People of the Universe: *Líně s tebou spím / Lazy Love. In Memoriam Milan Hlavsa*, Praha: Globus Music, 2001.

Krejcarová, Jana: *A Letter [Dopis Egonu Bondymu]*, with "An introduction to her life and work" by A. G. Brain; in: *Yazzyk Magazine* 2, Prague, 1993.

Kubínová, Pavlína (ed.): *Tschechische Schriftsteller / Czech Writers*, Prague: Ministry of Culture of the Czech Republic, 2001.

Libánský, Abbé Jaroslav: *My Underground. Rodinné fotoalbum – Family Album – Familienfotoalbum 1972/82*, Vienna: Institut für culturresistante Güter, 2004.

Literature and Politics in Central Europe: Studies in Honour of Marketa Goetz-Stankiewicz. Editors: Leslie Miller, Klaus Petersen, Peter Stenberg, Karl

Zaenkel [See the text by Vilém Prečan: "Independent Literature and Samizdat in Czechoslovakia".], Camden House, Columbia, SC, USA, 1993.

Machovec, Martin: "Czech Underground Literature, 1969–1989: a Challenge to Textual Studies", in: *Voice, Text, Hypertext: Emerging Practices in Textual Studies*. Ed. Raimonda Modiano, Leroy F. Searle, Peter Schillingsburg; Seattle–London: Walter Chapin Simpson Center for the Humanities – University of Washington Press, 2004.

Machovec, Martin: "Czech Underground Musicians in Search of Art Innovation", in *East Central Europe* 38, (Leiden: Brill, 2008) 221–237.

Machovec, Martin: "Ideological Orientation and Political Views and Standpoints of Representatives of Czech Underground Culture, 1969–1989 (Underground and Dissidence – Allies or Enemies?)", in *eSamizdat* *2010-2011* (VIII), 177–188.

Machovec, Martin: "The Types and Functions of Samizdat Publications in Czechoslovakia, 1948–1989", in *Poetics Today*, No 1, Vol 30, Spring 2009, 1–26.

Machovec, Martin: "Underground and 'Under-the-Ground'. The standpoints of the underground community in Czech society in the 1970s and 1980 and the specific values of the underground culture", in *Behind the Iron Curtain. Review of the Institute for the Study of Totalitarian Regimes*, Czech Republic, No 4, 2016, 70–79.

Morganová, Pavlína: *Czech Action Art. Happenings, Actions, Events, Land Art, Body Art and Performance Art Behind the Iron Curtain*, Prague: Karolinum Press, 2014.

Naughton, James D. (ed.): *Eastern & Central Europe. Traveller's Literary Companion*; Brighton: In Print Publishing Ltd, 1995.

O'Connor, Rory: "Jailhouse Rock: In the Eastern European Underground, Making Music Can Be Downright Dangerous" [An Interview with Karel Voják], in *Mother Jones* magazine, May 1979, see: http://www.mediachannel.org/ news/reports/jailhouse.shtml/.

Porter, Robert: *Comedies of Defiance. An Introduction to Twentieth-Century Czech Fiction*; Brighton–Portland: Sussex Academic Press, 2001.

Prečan, Vilém et al.: "Bibliography of the Czechoslovak Samizdat. Samizdat periodicals 1977–1988", in: ACTA, vol. 2, no. 5–8, Winter 1988 (Scheinfeld: Dokumentationzentrum).

Prečan, Vilém: *Independent Literature and Samizdat in Czechoslovakia* [a catalogue to the exhibition V.Z.D.O.R. Výstava nezávislé literatury v samizdatu a exilu 1948–1989, Prague: Památník národního písemnictví, 1992], Ústav pro soudobé dějiny Československé akademie věd, Československé dokumentační středisko nezávislé literatury Prague: Scheinfeld-Schwarzenberg, 1992.

Primary Documents. A Sourcebook for Eastern and Central European Art since the 1950s. Ed. Laura Hoptman and Tomáš Pospiszyl; Foreword by Ilya Kabakov, New York: The Museum of Modern Art, 2002.

Pytlík, Radko: *The Sad King of Czech Literature Bohumil Hrabal. His Life and Work*; translated by Kathleen Hayes; Prague: Emporius, 2000.

Ságl, Jan: *Tanec na dvojitém ledě / Dancing on the Double Ice*, Prague: Kant, 2013.

Samizdat. Alternative Culture in Central and Eastern Europe from the 1960s to the 1980s. [a catalogue to an exhibition] Ed. Heidrun Hamersky [Contributors: Václav Havel, György Konrád, Vilém Prečan, László Rajk, Wolfgang Eichwede]; Bremen: The Research Centre for East European Studies at the University of Bremen, 2002.

Sanders, Edward: *A Visit to Prague. For the Prague Writers' Festival 2005*, Prague: Haštalská a.s. Hotel Josef, 2005.

Sedláčková Gibbs, Helena: *Moral Politics and Its Others: The Charter 77 Dissident Movement in Czechoslovakia (1977-1989).* A dissertation submitted at Department of Comparative Literature, New York University, May 2003. [See Chapter 1: "Charter 77 and Moral Politics".]

Serafin, Steven (ed.): *Twentieth-Century Eastern European Writers. Third Series*, Detroit–San Francisco–London–Boston–Woodbridge: Gale Group, 2001.

Skilling, Gordon H.: *Charter 77 and Human Rights in Czechoslovakia*, London: Allen and Unwin, 1981. [See Chapter: "Musical Underground".]

Skilling, Gordon H.: *Samizdat and an Independent Society in Central and Eastern Europe*, Oxford: Macmillan Press, 1989; Columbus: Ohio State University Press, 1989. [See Part II, Chapter 4 - "Other Independent Currents".]

Svoboda, Vladislav "Hendrix" [correctly: Smetana, Vladimír "Hendrix"]: *Od dospívání k dozpívání / When the Singing had to Stop*, in: *Pope Smoked Dope / Papež kouřil trávu. Rocková hudba a alternativní vizuální kultura 60. let / Rock music and the alternative visual culture of the 1960s.* [a catalogue to an exhibition], Prague: Kant, 2005.

Steiner, Peter: *The Deserts of Bohemia. Czech Fiction and Its Social Context*; Ithaca–London: Cornell University Press, 2000.

The Merry Ghetto [a booklet/catalogue added to the record *The Plastic People... Prague. Egon Bondy's Happy Hearts Club Banned*], London–Paris: Boží Mlýn & SCOPA Invisible Production © and The Plastic People Defense Fund, 1978. [Lyrics and texts by Egon Bondy, Pavel Zajíček, Josef Vondruška, Svatopluk Karásek, Milan Koch, Miroslav Skalický, František Vaněček, Václav Havel, Ivan Hartel, Jan Patočka, Ivan M. Jirous.]

The Plastic People of the Universe [texts of the songs, chronology, discography etc.], Prague: Globus Music–Maťa, 1999. [Lyrics and texts by Ivan Jirous, Michal Jernek, Jiří Kolář, Egon Bondy, Vratislav Brabenec, Ladislav Klíma, Fanda Pánek, Ivan Wernisch, Petr Placák, Pavel Zajíček etc. translated by Olga Záhorbenská, Paul Wilson, Jan Jonák, Marek Tomin, Josef Janda.]

Topol, Jáchym: *Game Park* [*Obora*], a poem; translated by A. G. Brain; in: *Yazzyk Magazine* 4, Prague, 1995.

Tucker, Aviezer: *The Philosophy and Politics of Czech Dissidence from Patočka to Havel*, Pittsburgh: University of Pittsburgh Press, 2000. [See Chapter 5 – "The Meaning of Dissidence and Charter 77", Part "The Parallel Polis".]

Tuckerová, Veronika: "The Remains of the Triple Ghetto in the Prague Underground," *Brucken. Germanistisches Jahrbuch TSCHECHIEN-SLOWAKEI 2015 / Germanic Yearbook CZECH REPUBLIC-SLOVAKIA 2015*, 23/1–2 (2015), Prague: DAAD, Nakladatelství Lidové noviny 2016, 193–210.

Vanicek, Anna Naninka: *Passion Play: Underground Rock Music in Czechoslovakia 1968–1989*, North York: York University, 1997.

Vladislav, Jan (ed.): *Václav Havel or Living in Truth*, London: Faber and Faber, 1986.

Yanosik, Joseph: *The Plastic People of the Universe*, March 1996, see: http://www.furious.com/perfect/pulnoc.html/.

Zajíček, Pavel: *DG 307 - gift to the shadows* (*fragment*), Uppsala: Šafrán and Boží Mlýn, 1982. [The leaflet added to the record contains some of Zajíček's lyrics translated into English.]

Zajíček, Pavel: *DG 307 - SVĚDEK SPÁLENÝHO ČASU 1979/1980* [5CD], Louny: Guerilla Records, 2013. [The booklets added to the CDs contain all of Zajíček's lyrics released with music on them, both in Czech and in English translation (by Marek Tomin).]

Underground music

AKTUAL - ATENTÁT NA KULTURU, ed. Jaroslav Riedel, Prague: Anne Records, 2003.

AKTUAL - DĚTI BOLŠEVIZMU, Louny: Guerilla Records, 2005.

BÍLÉ SVĚTLO - DĚLNÍCI BÍLÉHO SVĚTLA, ed. Vladimír Lábus Drápal, Louny: Guerilla Records, 2006.

CHARLIE SOUKUP - GENERACE, Globus Music, Praha, 2001.

CHARLIE SOUKUP - RADIO, eds. Martin Machovec - Karel Kourek, Prague: Galén, 2012.

DG 307 - GIFT TO THE SHADOWS (FRAGMENT), Uppsala: Šafrán and Boží Mlýn, 1982.

DG 307 - 1973-1975 [LP], Prague: Globus International, 1991.

DG 307 - DAR STÍNŮM (JARO 1979), *PTÁK UTRŽENEJ ZE ŘETĚZU* (PODZIM 1979), *TORZO* (LÉTO 1980) [3 CD], Prague: Globus International, 1993.

DG 307 - HISTORIE HYSTERIE. Archiv dochovaných nahrávek 1973-75 [2 CD], ed. Jaroslav Riedel, Louny: Guerilla Records, 2004.

DG 307 - SVĚDEK SPÁLENÝHO ČASU 1979/1980 [5CD], Louny: Guerilla Records, 2013.

JIM ČERT - SVĚTLU VSTŘÍC, Prague: Aske Globus International, 1990.

JIM ČERT - POUTNÍK Z TRANSPORTY, Prague: Puky Records, 1997.

SVATOPLUK KARÁSEK - SAY NO TO THE DEVIL, Uppsala: Šafrán 78 and Boží Mlýn, 1979.

SVATOPLUK KARÁSEK - ŘEKNI ĎÁBLOVI NE (1978), ed. Jaroslav Riedel, Prague: Globus International, 1998.

SVATOPLUK KARÁSEK - RÁNY ZNÍ (BLUES, SPIRITUALS & ...), Prague: Globus Music, 2000.

SVATOPLUK KARÁSEK - ŘEKNI ĎÁBLOVI NE [2 CD], eds Jaroslav Riedel - Karel Kourek, Prague: Galén, 2012.

THE PLASTIC PEOPLE OF THE UNIVERSE I. Muž bez uší (1969-1972), ed. Jaroslav Riedel, Prague: Globus Music, 2002.

THE PLASTIC PEOPLE OF THE UNIVERSE II. Vožralej jak slíva (koncerty 1973-75), ed. Jaroslav Riedel, Prague: Globus Music, 1997.

THE PLASTIC PEOPLE OF THE UNIVERSE III. Egon Bondy's Happy Hearts Club Banned (1974-75), ed. Jaroslav Riedel, Prague: Globus Music, 2001.

THE PLASTIC PEOPLE OF THE UNIVERSE IV. Ach to státu hanobení (koncerty 1976-77), ed. Jaroslav Riedel, Prague: Globus Music, 2000.

THE PLASTIC PEOPLE OF THE UNIVERSE V. Pašijové hry velikonoční (1978), ed. Jaroslav Riedel, Prague: Globus Music, 1998.

THE PLASTIC PEOPLE OF THE UNIVERSE VI. Jak bude po smrti (1979), ed. Jaroslav Riedel, Prague: Globus Music, 1998.

THE PLASTIC PEOPLE OF THE UNIVERSE VII. Co znamená vésti koně (1981), ed. Jaroslav Riedel, Prague: Globus Music, 2002.

THE PLASTIC PEOPLE OF THE UNIVERSE VIII. Kolejnice duní (1977–82), ed. Jaroslav Riedel, Prague: Globus Music, 2000.

THE PLASTIC PEOPLE OF THE UNIVERSE IX. Hovězí porážka (1983–84), ed. Jaroslav Riedel, Prague: Globus Music, 1997.

THE PLASTIC PEOPLE OF THE UNIVERSE X. Půlnoční myš (1985–86), ed. Jaroslav Riedel, Prague: Globus Music, 2001.

THE PLASTIC PEOPLE OF THE UNIVERSE XI. Trouble Every Day, ed. Jaroslav Riedel, Prague: Globus Music, 2002. [including bonus: the PPU discography, lyrics in Czech and English, photos]

THE PLASTIC PEOPLE OF THE UNIVERSE & AGON ORCHESTRA – Pašijové hry / Passion Play, Prague: Knihy Hana, 2004.

THE PLASTIC PEOPLE OF THE UNIVERSE: Do lesíčka na čekanou 1. 12. 1973 [2CD], Guerilla Records, Louny, 2006.

THE PLASTIC PEOPLE OF THE UNIVERSE & AGON ORCHESTRA – Obešel já polí pět. Koncert na počest Ladislava Klímy (2003), [2CD], ed. Jaroslav Riedel, Louny: Guerilla Records, 2009.

THE PLASTIC PEOPLE OF THE UNIVERSE. Komplet nahrávek 1969–2004, ed Jaroslav Riedel [2 DVD comprising the music on CDs I.-XI. + PPU: Bez ohňů je underground (concert 1992) + PPU concert 1997 + PPU Líně s tebou spím / Lazy Love (2001) + PPU & Agon Orchestra – Pašijové hry (2004)], Prague: Levné knihy 2008.

UMĚLÁ HMOTA: BARBARA [LP], Prague: Globus International, 1991.

UMĚLÁ HMOTA II. VE SKLEPĚ – 1976/77 [2 CD] ed. Vladimír Lábus Drápal, Louny: Guerilla Records, 2003.

VONDRUŠKA JOSEF: THE DOM & UMĚLÁ HMOTA III – ROCK'N'ROLLOVÝ MILÁČEK [2CD], eds. Vladimír Drápal, Martin Machovec, Štěpán Smetáček, Louny: Guerilla Records, 2010.

20 minut z Říše [a TV documentary about I. M. Jirous]; dir. Václav Kučera; Czech Television (ČT), 1994.

Alternativní kultura I. [a 13-part TV documentary; on underground poetry: parts 4, 5, 6: *Od avantgardy do podzemí, Od undergroundu k šedé zóně, Ke konci věčných časů*], dir. Petr Slavík; Czech Television (ČT), 1998.

Alternativní kultura II. [an 11-part TV documentary; on underground poetry: parts 4 and 5; – *Poezie v podzemí I.*, *Poezie v podzemí II.*]; dir. Petr Slavík; Czech Television (ČT), 2003.

Atentát na kulturu [a TV propaganda documentary, condemning and vilifying Czech underground culture], dir. not mentioned, probably Ladislav Chocholoušek; Czechoslovak Television (ČST), 1977.

Bigbít [a 25-part TV documentary; on underground music: parts 24, 25], dir. Václav Křístek; Czech Television (ČT), 1998.

CONCERT, (*Premiéra*) [a documentary TV film (FATE): presenting the underground festival in Postupice, September 1974; accompanied by statements from participants (1990)], dir. Josef Dlouhý; Czechoslovak Television (ČST), 1990.

ČARODĚJ OZ / PIGI-FILMY [4 DVD with 22 featured and documentary films, 1980–1987; directors: Lubomír "Čaroděj" Drožď and Irena "Pigi" Gosmanová; with a booklet], ed. Martin Blažíček; Prague: FAMU/PAF Edition, 2012.

Fenomén underground [a 40-part TV documentary on underground culture, especially music and life style], directors: Břetislav Rychlík, Jana Chytilová, Jiří Fiedor, Václav Křístek; Czech Television (ČT), 2012.

Fišer alias Bondy [a TV documentary], dir. Jordi Niubo; Czech Television (ČT), 2000.

My žijeme v Praze [a documentary featuring Egon Bondy, 1984–85], directors Tomáš Mazal and Pavel "Pablo" Veselý; released on a DVD + CD: Egon Bondy: My žijeme v Praze..., Louny: Guerilla Records, 2007.

O kočkách, beatnicích a všeličems jiném [a TV documentary: M. Dohnal's interview with Bohumil Hrabal talking about Vladimír Boudník and Egon Bondy, 1966]; dir. Rudolf Růžička, FTF AMU, Prague, 1966.

Revolver Revue – 5 let pod zemí, 5 let na zemi, dir. Eva Koutná; Czech Television (ČT), 1996.

Samizdat [a 15-part TV documentary; on underground/samizdat literature, part 1 – *Padesátá léta*, part 6 – *Další samizdatové edice 70. a 80. let*, part 11 – *Undergroundový samizdat*]; dir. Andrej Krob; Czech Television (ČT), 2002.

Sie sass im Glashaus und warf mit Steinen. Ein Film von Nadja Seelich und Bernd Neuburger [an Austrian TV documentary about the life of Jana Krejcarová, featuring Egon Bondy, Ivo Vodseďálek, Johanna Kohnová, and others]; dir. Nadja Seelich; EXTRAFILM, 1992.

The Plastic People of the Universe [a documentary film, with English subtitles]; dir. Jana Chytilová; Czech Television (ČT) and Video 57, 2001.

The Plastic People of the Universe 1969–1985. Více než 2 hodiny autentických dokumentů [DVD with 12 documentaries; directors: César de Ferrari, Jan Špáta, Petr Prokeš, Jan Ságl, Josef Dlouhý, František Stárek "Čuňas", Tomáš Liška, Aleš Havlíček, Lubomír Drožď, Jan Kašpar etc.], Prague: Levné knihy, 2011.

Vlasatý svět uprostřed holohlavé republiky [a TV documentary about the hippie youth in Czechoslovakia in the late 1960s]; dir. Tomáš Škrdlant, Angelika Haunerová; Czech Television (ČT), 1994.

Zblízka: Vis Magor [a TV documentary on I. M. Jirous], dir. Andrej Krob; Czech Television (ČT), 1999.

Z Ruzyně do New Yorku [a documentary on the conference on Czech literature held at New York University, 1990], dir. Jitka Pistoriusová, Czechoslovak Television [ČST], 1990.

Egon Bondy (1930-2007), poet, prose writer, philosopher, and historian of philosophy, started writing in the late 1940s and with his friends established one of the first samizdat editions as early as 1951. He soon became a legend of this early phase of Czech underground culture, and later strongly influenced the new wave in the development of it, following the year 1968. Bondy was one of the most prolific and fruitful Czech underground writers, but his activities were often somewhat controversial. After 1989 his works started being published in Czechoslovakia (later: Czech Republic and Slovakia) and nowadays they are available in more than 50 volumes, including the commented edition of his collected poetry in three volumes: *Básnické spisy*, 2014-2016, and his complete philosophical essays in four volumes: *Filosofické dílo*, 2007-2013.

Ivan Martin "Magor" Jirous (1944-2011) is the most important figure of the Czech underground culture of 1970s and without much exaggeration it can be said that without Jirous' stubborn effort the underground community and its literary and musical output would never become reality. Jirous was also an excellent essayist and poet and as a result of his activities gained reputation as one of the most often prosecuted and terrorized political prisoners in Czechoslovakia of 70s and 80s. Jirous' complete poetical works finally came out in three volumes in 2015 under the title *Magorova summa*, but between 1989-2011 he published a number of collections of poems for which he was awarded Jaroslav Seifert Prize. His essays and reviews came out in 1997 in a volume *Magorův zápisník* (*Magor's Diary*).

The poet and prose writer **Jáchym Topol** (*1962) is one of the best-known representatives of the "second underground generation" in Czechoslovakia. Topol co-founded the samizdat literary and art journal *Revolver Revue* in 1985 which during the five years of its illegal existence became one of the best samizdat periodicals in pre November '89 Czechoslovakia. Thanks to Topol and his contemporaries older underground artists, writers, and musicians found a common platform with the younger ones, and also with a number of dissidents who previously had known little about the underground of rock musicians. Today, Topol is one of the most renowned Czech writers and a number of books he wrote after 1989 were translated into foreign languages, including his bestseller *City Sister Silver* (in English in 2000).

The fourth author in this volume is the Canadian **Paul Wilson** (*1941), translator, essayist and once a rock musician, who spent ten years in Czechoslovakia (1967–1977) where he made friends with underground musicians, writers, and artists, and himself took part in their activities. He learned Czech and when he was banished from the country in 1977 he returned to Canada where during the following years he did a lot to support Czech underground culture. Thanks to Wilson the first Plastic People album *Egon Bondy's Happy Hearts Club Banned* was released in France and England in 1978 – to be followed by a number of other musical releases. Wilson wrote about the Czech underground and soon started translating texts of Czech writers that could not come out in their home country before 1989 – e.g. Václav Havel and Bohumil Hrabal. An anthology of his essays in Czech translation came out in Prague in 2011 under the English title *Bohemian Rhapsodies*.

INDEX OF NAMES*

*⁾ Names in Bibliography, Discography and the list of Documentary Films are not included.

The modern history of Central Europe is notable for its political and cultural discontinuities and often violent changes as well as its attempts to preserve and (re) invent traditional cultural identities. This series cultivates contemporary translations of influential literary works that have been unavailable to a global readership due to censorship, the effects of the Cold War and the frequent political disruptions in Czech publishing and its international ties. Readers of English, in today's cosmopolitan Prague and anywhere in the physical and electronic world, can now become acquainted with works that capture the Central European historical experience. Works that helped express and form Czech and Central European identity, humour and imagination. Believing that any literary canon can be defined only in dialogue with other cultures, the series publishes classics, often used in Western university courses, as well as (re)discoveries aiming to provide new perspectives in intermedial studies of literature, history and culture. All titles are accompanied by an afterword. Translations are reviewed and circulated in the global scholarly community before publication – this is reflected by our nominations for several literary awards.

Modern Czech Classics series edited by Karolinum Press

Published titles
Zdeněk Jirotka: Saturnin (2003, 2005, 2009, 2013; pb 2016)
Vladislav Vančura: Summer of Caprice (2006; pb 2016)
Karel Poláček: We Were a Handful (2007; pb 2016)
Bohumil Hrabal: Pirouettes on a Postage Stamp (2008)
Karel Michal: Everyday Spooks (2008)
Eduard Bass: The Chattertooth Eleven (2009)
Jaroslav Hašek: Behind the Lines. Bugulma and Other Stories (2012; pb 2016)
Bohumil Hrabal: Rambling On (2014; pb 2016)
Ladislav Fuks: Of Mice and Mooshaber (2014)
Josef Jedlička: Midway Upon the Journey of Our Life (2016)
Jaroslav Durych: God's Rainbow (2016)
Ladislav Fuks: The Cremator (2016)
Bohuslav Reynek: The Well at Morning (2017)
Viktor Dyk: The Pied Piper (2017)

Forthcoming
Jiří R. Pick: Society for the Prevention of Cruelty to Animals
Ludvík Vaculík: Czech Dreambook
Jan Čep: Short Stories